MW01603117

Passages...
through grief

Healing Life's Losses

Leader's Guide

Mary Ann Lippincott, Ph.D.
Susan H. Williams, GC-C

Copyright © 2015 Mary Ann Lippincott and Susan H. Williams.

All rights reserved. No part of this book may be reproduced, stored, or transmitted by any means—whether auditory, graphic, mechanical, or electronic—without written permission of both publisher and author, except in the case of brief excerpts used in critical articles and reviews. Unauthorized reproduction of any part of this work is illegal and is punishable by law.

ISBN: 978-1-4834-3660-9 (sc)
ISBN: 978-1-4834-3659-3 (e)

Because of the dynamic nature of the Internet, any web addresses or links contained in this book may have changed since publication and may no longer be valid. The views expressed in this work are solely those of the author and do not necessarily reflect the views of the publisher, and the publisher hereby disclaims any responsibility for them.

Lulu Publishing Services rev. date: 10/20/2015

Dedicated to
John Cary Williams
and
Dorothy C. Lippincott

Mission Statement

Passages...through grief provides opportunities
to learn about the grief process,
develop skills for healing,
and complete what is unfinished
within a respectful and supportive environment.

Table of Contents for Leader's Guide

Opening Statements

The Leader

Mindset and Framework

Set-up Needs

Promoting the Program

Passages...through grief Creators

Mary Ann Lippincott, Ph.D.

Licensed Clinical Psychologist (VA); Fellow, American Association of Pastoral Counselors; American Association of Marital and Family Therapists (former Clinical Member); and National Certified Counselor. Mary Ann has worked with grieving people as a counselor and psychotherapist since 1978 and began with the group forerunner of *Passages... through grief* in 2000.

Susan H. Williams, BSW, GC-C

As a Certified Grief Counselor, Susan served as a coordinator and facilitator of Compassionate Friends of Central Virginia (10 years) and a Resolve Through Sharing Bereavement Counselor (10 years). With a Bachelor of Social Work she has worked with grieving people as a counselor both individually and in groups since 1991. She began serving as a leader of *Passages...through grief* in 2006. She resides in Lynchburg, VA where she works as a Hospice social worker and a youth minister.

In Appreciation

A number of people assisted us in bringing this program to fruition.

Our appreciation goes to Marilyn Dickson for her *Grief Recovery* manual which has served as the forerunner and inspiration for ***Passages...through grief***. Like Marilyn, we see ourselves as instruments and encouragers toward the goal of healing the griefs in people's lives. More gratitude goes to Larry Yeagley who generously allowed us to reprint chapters from his book *Grief Recovery* as supplements to sessions. His work is back in print, and we recommend it to grievers.

We would also like to thank Kris Shabestar, Sandy McCann, Cathy Foote, and Amy Moore for sharing their particular gifts. We appreciate our families for their loving support in this project.

Preface

The ***Passages...through grief*** program evolved out of many years of working with grieving people. We have listened to their journeys, recognized their struggles and strengths, learned what is helpful and hurtful, and admired their courage. We have been blessed to have the education and knowledge to put what we have learned into a program that serves to guide grievers through a process of healing.

Passages...through grief addresses issues in a systematic and practical way. By coming to understand how grief operates, participants are encouraged to work through the feelings of grief, to develop skills to use in the process, and to complete the incompleteness of their loss. In addition, those who are active in partaking of the program's educational component find there is assistance in understanding grief and healing overall. They come to recognize how the process works through their thoughts, feelings and relationships. Progressively, they are supported in their efforts to process through the varied aspects of their personal grief journey.

This program is unique in that it provides a group experience for those having all types of losses. We have found that the type of loss is not as significant as the responses to grief, which are similar. The combination of a variety of losses enables the leaders and participants to publically recognize that loss, in any form, has power. Respect for the loss is demonstrated by an accepting, nonjudgmental attitude where no comparison of losses is permitted for leaders or participants. One finds that the type of loss does not matter in the long run, for much of the journey is similar among people.

We have been gifted by the many people who have moved through this program. May you feel gifted as well.

Introduction for Leaders

Hello, Leader. This guide is for you. In these pages, we want to offer the mindset and framework to make the *Passages...through grief* a workable program for you and the participants you serve. The articles here give explanation for the grief education pieces in the program and facilitate your clarification of the exercises. We also seek to share supportive "how to" information for your understanding and ideas to encourage participants. They need to sense that the leader can confirm why they hurt so badly and give hope when they see nothing valuable for their future.

We wholeheartedly believe in healing from grief. This becomes clear to the people who come to *Passages...through grief* as they seek hope. They count on our conviction until they can come to believe it for themselves.

We encourage you to spend time with each other as leaders so that your trust in working together upholds you personally and strengthens you as a team. Be prepared to grow emotionally and spiritually yourselves. You will have many opportunities. Working with grieving people is a privilege. Their stories are treasures. They entrust their tenderness and vulnerability to us at a crux time in their lives. We always need to be mindful of that trust and handle it with care.

As you use this program, make it your own with personal examples and the particular abilities you have to offer.

Blessings for the journey.

Leadership Requirements

Each *Passages...through grief* program requires one or two leaders. Additional facilitators may be utilized to lead small groups, known as "sharing groups." The number of leaders and facilitators is dependent on the number of participants. The leaders will serve as a team for all large group activities. When the participants divide into sharing groups, one leader or facilitator will go with each group. Each sharing group should not exceed eight.

Prior to Session One

It is necessary for all leaders and facilitators to meet prior to the beginning of the *Passages...through grief* program to review all curriculum and define roles of leadership. To be successful, the leaders and facilitators must understand how important it is to work as a team and be supportive of each other. They will have an additional responsibility to discuss "Red Flags."

Groups

The whole group meets together for the foundations portion of each session. Then, the group is divided by the leaders into sharing groups, each of which includes a balance of types of losses, challenging personalities, males, females, and ethnicity.

Post Session Meeting

After each session, it is necessary for leaders and facilitators to process the experience together. The content should include items listed in that week's "Schedule for Leaders."

Leadership Qualities

The success of the program experience relies on the qualities of the leadership. Leaders and facilitators for *Passages...through grief* need to have both the qualities of a teacher and a counselor. It is important for leaders and facilitators to have dealt with and resolved a personal grief experience. In order to be effective, the leaders and facilitators must exhibit the following characteristics and abilities:

- Knowledge of the grief process
- Understanding of group process and dynamics (see "Sharing Groups")
- Openness to the variety of grief responses and experiences
- Have access to a trained professional for consultation and referrals (see "Red Flags")
- Understanding of the *Passages...through grief* material
- Commitment to present the *Passages...through grief* material as written
- Ability to clarify the written materials, to prepare, and use fitting examples
- Ability to provide empathetic, accepting, and nonjudgmental listening
- Ability to actively listen, clarify, paraphrase, and validate participants' statements
- Commitment to not comparing losses
- Ability to engage participants with humor
- Must not project thoughts, experiences, or feelings onto others
- Grounded—must be able to sustain oneself and show no visible reaction while witnessing participants' anguish
- Recognition that participants come with one loss but discover other loss(es) requiring attention
- Enthusiastic support and encouragement for the activities outlined in the program

Assignments that Require a Listener

In the directions for assignments "My Loss History," "Charting the Relationship," and "Letter of Declaration" (Sessions Three, Four and Five,) the participants are asked to share their writings aloud with another person. Hearing their own voice makes their story more real and valid. Leaders need to strongly emphasize the value of sharing assignments with another, as most participants shy away from this task.

The listener must be a person who is able to hear the assignments unconditionally and without judgment. This may limit the list of listeners. Not every participant may have someone with whom to share. If this is the case, we suggest they ask their *Passages... through grief* leader, a pastor, or another professional to be their listener.

All I Can Do is Listen

We have often heard this comment from **Passages...through grief** participants. They long for release from the grief. They want to make the grief subside for each other. Yet even as they are noting the relief felt from sharing their own struggles with the group and "feeling heard," there is a subtle disconnect with the actual power of listening itself. As leaders, it is vital that we are continually clear about the healing effects of listening - in our role, as well as the power listening has among the participants.

As the program progresses, we often recall how challenging it was for these people to walk into the first session. They relate stories of how vulnerable they felt. Weeks later, they recognize that the fear of opening up and being known has gradually become crucial to their healing journey. The connection is made emotionally for each person. At the same time, the connections among grievers are then becoming more and more supportive, and we all sense the tide turning. Participants enter the sessions with friendly tidings and caring questions for the others' week. Even if one is more quiet and reluctant to share openly, they are watching. They are witnessing a healing process in action. They will later note how they want to keep trying for themselves.

For the leaders, Sessions Four, Five and Six are a time of an unfolding of struggle, growth, and healing. We soak up the privilege of accompanying these grievers on their journey. Invariably, we learn from them every time.

We leaders need to be very clear about what we have to learn from grievers. First, we must enter into our listening to them openly, setting aside preconceived notions of how their story goes. This can be a challenge when we have heard a number of loss stories or have been through a similar loss ourselves. Grievers speak a few sentences, and we can be ready to "take off" on helping them along. It is difficult to sit with the pain and really be with them. However, there is probably nothing more imperative to assisting a griever than to listen without ready solutions. We tell them each grief is unique. By listening, we have the privilege of witnessing their experience, their feelings, their concerns and helplessness. By listening, we demonstrate our trust in them and in the healing process. The teaching piece of **Passages...through grief** allows participants to glean understanding of how to process and claim skills they can apply to their specific grief experience.

Other learning comes to leaders as we observe participants active in their grief journey. We perceive how the process works uniquely for each one as they discover what it takes to heal. For one, it may be revisiting family relationships that need sorting out and healing. For another, writing the details of their grief feelings in letters to the lost one can bring about a transformation of their spirit and the ongoing connection with the lost one. The surprising gifts of healing are always gratifying. At the hopeful point for many, when they want to give the leaders the credit for their progress, it is important to remind them of their part in the process and the hard work they have accomplished.

Red Flags

When dealing with an assortment of people in a group, one always needs to be alert to how they come together. The leaders need to be ready to work with each unique mix in order to facilitate the best possible outcome. Grief, as any crisis, exacerbates individuals' reactivity. It is, therefore, important to be attuned to behaviors that may interfere with the ***Passages...through grief*** experience for individuals as well as the group as a whole. Groups can generally tolerate and sympathize with some unusual behavior. However, other behaviors can interfere, particularly in the small group, where participants are invited to openly share their feelings and experiences. Common interfering behaviors are as follows:

The non-invested participant - When one member is not actively doing assignments, not responsive in group or is quiet in sharing group, their unavailability affects the trust within the circle. Sharing groups are pulled back when sharing is not mutual. In other words, silence is not golden. This participant may need to be approached outside the session to see how they might be brought along.

The over-talker - When one member is so focused on talking and not listening in turn, there is lack of space for others to feel invited to share of themselves. The over-talker must be redirected by the facilitator. If this is not effective in the small group, it must be addressed privately.

The psychologically vulnerable one - When a leader is concerned for a participant's safety or possible loss of control, it is imperative to be proactive. It is the leader's responsibility to have a private talk with this person to make an assessment, if that lies in their capacity, or to provide resources for immediate professional help. It is clearly reassuring to have such resources at the ready, so the leader and the facilitators can know there is an emergency plan.

The absorbing participant – When a participant focuses on the pain and/or loss of another in a way that distracts them from their own work, it can be uncomfortable to others in the sharing group. This also functions as a deflection from the work they need to be doing. This is closely related to comparison of losses and needs to be addressed in the group.

Why Do We Use the Butterfly?

The butterfly is used in *Passages...through grief* as a logo, as well as a metaphor for the transformation healing can bring grievers.

When we see a butterfly, we see a colorful, beautiful winged creature that looks rather fragile. We don't think of the egg, caterpillar or chrysalis—the forms it has evolved through to become that amazing being. Nor do we note the sticky, hard work it requires through the metamorphosis process.

In the program, we demonstrate that participants' healing takes work and focus, too. We encourage a similar change aspiration for grievers...to go through the natural and difficult steps of healing, to evolve and be able to fly again. The butterfly may appear fragile, but it is sturdy.

People enter the grief process with different strengths and challenges. One may come at an "egg stage" and have a great deal to accomplish in order to progress, like those who have had difficult upbringings or lack support systems. Others may not have knowledge of the grief process, and that it is normal. There are many hindrances. So there may be much to accomplish along with the grieving itself. Some butterflies get stuck in the process. In fact, some people decide to repeat the *Passages...through grief* program. Another participant may just need some information and group support; they could be considered at a "chrysalis stage," ready to use the program as a spur to growth so they can fly. We welcome people where they are and encourage them to personalize the program to meet their own needs.

Several other metaphors are used throughout the program in order to make the facets of healing relatable. It is our thinking that much of the work of grief is simple and natural, though very difficult to take on for the griever. Therefore, we have found that using metaphors like the butterfly, cleaning out a closet, or healing a wound make sense to people and can be easily recalled as they encourage themselves in the everyday work of healing.

The butterfly is our inspiration—a creature that demonstrates how metamorphosis works. There are obvious parallels for grieving and healing, we readily use. We see people who have journeyed through a trauma or a loss and been transformed to a stronger, healthier, more vibrant person. We admire and we wonder, how did they do that? They can tell us. And their witness is inspirational.

What Society Says About Grieving

In the 19th century, the grief traditions in America established a firm understanding and acceptance of the cycle of life and death. People were cared for in the home through illness or accidents, and usually died at home. The body was on display for all to see. There were opportunities to give a final touch, a kiss on the cheek. At the funeral, grievers were free to wail, keen and mourn openly. Everyone, including children, witnessed death as a normal part of life. Grievers wore black for each death, oftentimes wearing black for much of their adult lives as they claimed grief for each member of their family. This visual statement encouraged others to acknowledge the loss. This acceptance of death was a natural part of life, although the feelings and expressions of grief were not encouraged.

Society has gradually moved away from these traditions to current practices. With modern medical advancements, we are living longer lives. Death is often viewed as an enemy that medicine should be able to beat. Our elderly and ill are generally cared for in hospitals or facilities rather than in the home. As a result, family and friends often do not take an active part in their care and only a few, if any, witness the death. At a funeral, the family is said to be "doing well" if they do not show emotion. The surviving immediate family members are given just three days off before being expected to return to work to resume their job with efficiency. If the death is of a loved friend or distant relative, no acknowledgement is given. Death has changed to now being seen as an uncomfortable, and often unacceptable, part of life.

Other losses lend themselves to a lack of acceptance as well. In a divorce, family and friends judge the situation and divide over who should be supported. A job is lost with empathy given to the unemployed for a few days but others move on, afraid it could happen to them. It is as if we do not want to see that others are grieving.

When people ask the griever, "How are you doing?" they often don't really want to hear the truth. The expectation from others is to move on and not show the pain. This results in leaving the griever in a place of loneliness and perhaps feeling a bit abnormal. It is then difficult to ask for support at this time of weakness. The silence of others is loud.

Doing Grief Work

Grief work is truly difficult. It affects all aspects of who we are mentally, intellectually, physically, emotionally, and spiritually (see Session One "Grief is a Process").

Most people do not know how to grieve. Some will come having had their first significant loss. Others may have suffered a significant life event, but have not completed their grief work, leaving them without the confidence and tools to process their responses effectively.

Having a loss turns the world upside down. What is familiar and comfortable is no more. It can be scary, intimidating and feel out of control. Most people just want to feel normal again, not knowing that their old normal no longer exists. This provides a challenge as a person is not comfortable within themselves. A new normal has to be developed through work and time. In the meantime, there is a void.

When the loss first happens, numbness provides a protection from feeling all the emotions at once. Then recognition of the loss seeps in. The mind works to accept what has happened and to manage the pain. What is lost is often idealized – it becomes better than it was, sometimes even perfect in the mind of the person grieving. Of course this is unrealistic, as no relationship is perfect. There is always conflict, whether spoken or not. It is necessary to help the person recognize what was - the good and the bad.

The old saying "life is not fair" becomes a reality. It's an up-in-your-face truth: life is not fair. The unfairness of grief takes work and processing to accept. It's not an easy task for many, particularly those who have a strong need to control.

Grief insists that you deal with a future without the person or situation. It is human to look forward, to set goals, to seek hope for the future. Loss takes that away. It leaves us without the ability to have time to be with that person or situation. It robs us of the chance to make changes. It denies us the hope of a different outcome.

Each person has a support network of friends, family, coworkers, and community. When a loss occurs, this network is challenged. Those who were counted upon before as the loss may not be able to provide the necessary support in this new situation. Some supporters are uncomfortable with grief themselves. They don't know what to say or don't understand how grief can feel. They just want the person to be healed, so they won't be faced with witnessing the pain. Most often family, friends and co-workers give the message that the person needs to move on. In essence, go back to who they used to be. And that can't happen.

It is vital for a grieving person to have at least one person who will travel with them on their journey. Someone is needed who will listen and not judge, who will not try to change, direct or minimize feelings. If a supportive person does not come forward from the original network, the griever may feel more abandoned and alone. Finding a support person is difficult but important to the process. Support through groups, professionals, clergy are all available, and the leader may need to offer guidance to these different options.

It is vital for the leaders to fully appreciate how difficult it can be for the participants to walk through the door of **Passages...through grief.** Witnessing their work and transformation from the first session to the last is humbling.

Taking Control

A key concept in doing the work of **Passages...through grief** is to help participants understand they have more control of their healing than they think they do (although less than they'd like). This seems simple, but for many it isn't. The feelings of grief are often huge and overwhelming. Taking control may be an unknown concept, be very intimidating, or feel beyond their reach.

Leaders and facilitators are charged with helping participants learn and recognize that they are able to affect their grief responses through the actions they take. We use "small steps" as a lead-in to gaining this sense of control. A "small step" equals taking action of any degree in the direction they want to go. This includes claiming feelings, processing, asserting oneself, and providing self-care. Participants may need help selecting specific "small steps." Encouragement and recognition from leaders and group members are rewarding and promote personal confidence. This leads to a sense of control in their healing.

Small steps also hold promise for the griever's long-term adjustment. A reference is made in Session One,"...to discover my emerging self through the grief process." Unless one has gone through grief in the past and learned grief's lessons, it is hard to comprehend that anything valuable can come from such pain. So no effort is made in the beginning of **Passages...through grief** to press for understanding of the whole concept of valuable change. Instead, we encourage participants to experience change through the "small steps" process. The leaders can encourage and support them in the discovery of their emerging self into a healthy new normal.

Cleaning out the Closet

When speaking of the grief process, it is useful to have everyday examples that are readily relatable. One metaphor we use is "cleaning out the closet." It goes; when we approach a jammed full closet, we know that all that stuff and clutter has to be removed before cleaning can begin. The stuff has to be removed and then sorted. In like manner, any grief has an assortment of experiences and memories that need to be brought to mind and sorted. Consciously, we have to recognize memories that are heavy and troublesome, that need some work in order to make them fit for our lives. Other memories will be pleasant and available for fond recall. The point is to consider the full variety of emotional elements of the loss and treat them with kind respect.

After the clutter of the closet has been sorted, the interior of the closet needs to be cleaned before it is refilled. As memory vessels, we need clearing and preparing, too. Ways to get prepared are found in the skills we focus on in *Passages...through grief,* like writing, sharing, and making use of the "Self-care: Relievers of Grief" (see Session Three). The phrase "gentle self-care" draws attention to the attitude we want to encourage for participants to use with themselves, and we repeat the phrase to them throughout the program.

Wound Concept

When we have a physical injury, we recognize that it needs tending. We don't ignore it or just slap a bandage on it, because we know there can be unwanted reactions or even dangerous infection without treatment. When it comes to loss in our lives, there is a parallel lesson to know and use.

Like the physical hurt which needs cleaning and treating, along with time to heal, the resolution of grief is a result of taking small steps. These small steps are a parallel for "cleaning out" our emotional wound and could include emotional releases, like crying, writing our acknowledged feelings, or talking to a trusted friend. It is valuable to recognize that we need to progress at a rate that will not overwhelm or interfere with a new-forming scab (a sign of healing).

The treatment refers to our identifying such specific actions we can decide to take that will be related to our loss. For example, a step could be driving by, then later revisiting the site of the loss, be it a hospital or former workplace.

As healing occurs for a deep or profound wound of grief, scarring takes place. In a physical injury the skin tissue develops a scar whose appearance is different and whose fiber stronger than uninjured skin. Likewise, an emotional scar forms during the healing process. This scar effect strengthens us in spiritual renewal and emotional growth...a visible sign of the very hard work of grief and healing.

Time + Work = Healing

Grieving the Unloved

A sympathy card arrives extolling the deceased and underscoring how missed this person is. The clear message is to hold dearly to the wonderful memories. Such a card is seen as a gift for those who have lost a **loved one.** But what does such a card do for one who has lost an **unloved one**?

Grief can be tricky business. What happens when a griever is feeling relief that their unloved one has finally gone? How can they voice the mix of anguish and liberation that bystanders don't want to hear? For this person, grief can be very difficult, complex, and lonely.

When there is loss of an unloved one, there is a huge load of unresolved relationship baggage including emotional, spiritual, and relational incompleteness—with no hope of resolution with the deceased. In order to address the layers of anguish, non-forgiveness, and unfinished business, the griever must become conscious and willing to work hard to resolve the loss. It isn't easy to garner that willingness, because it's a door that is difficult to open, and finding support for the process can be challenging. Most often the griever senses that they are not allowed, or at least not encouraged to speak how they really feel. It can be a lonesome walk.

The griever can feel not only alone, but somehow "wrong" in their loss reactions to the unloved one. Of course, they have many compatriots, but people aren't supposed to "speak ill of the dead," so the griever remains mum on the topic. Having worked with clients over the years trying to resolve grief of a difficult relationship, we wonder if Hallmark has missed a market for folks looking for greeting cards for the loss of an unloved person. It could be a money maker!

The leader can expect to regularly have participants who come with complex losses, replete with unresolved issues. The loss may be with someone who has died, or one who lives with divorce, or strained relationship(s). So instead of just focusing specifically on the death or divorce, the griever needs to be more involved with the quality of the relationship. In fact, the definition of grief we use in the program (see Session Two) takes this probability into account. The way the loss is experienced **will** be greatly effected by the experience of the relationship. This point is referred to throughout the program. Participants should be encouraged to allow the full range of feelings the relationship evokes, then to speak, write, or find a physical outlet.

Unsettled relationship baggage is often the element that blocks the healing process. Until it is dealt with, the griever can be stuck in unresolved grief. One of the key exercises in Session Four gives the griever a timeline to chart the positive as well as the difficult memories from the life of the relationship. Session Five is focused on the topic of forgiveness, which includes a letting-go ritual that is both poignant and releasing. Finally, we believe it is critical to acknowledge and facilitate the griever's old, painful relationship. Leaders should be clear in recognizing when a member's needs require more in-depth counseling and have referral resources available.

Most participants are focused on losses via death, divorce, or relationship strain. However, the leader needs to be open to a wider variety of losses that will bring people to **Passages...through grief** (see "Recognizing Losses").

When a potential participant contacts the leader to register for the program, the leader's affirmation of their particular loss can be a major first step in their owning it. As leaders, we need to regularly challenge ourselves to be attuned to where loss exists, so that we can facilitate the process of grieving.

Where's God in All This?

Frequently grief groups and programs put a loud emphasis on religious beliefs and practices. We in **Passages...through grief** take a different stance.

It is our experience that participants' reactions to God references vary, even among believers, during the grief process. Those who find their faith strengthened tend to speak openly in the group about that reaction—how much stronger their faith has grown during grief. Periodically, one of these folks may ask why we do not have prayer together. In our answer we respond by acknowledging their faith experience. But we go on to explain that for some people faith is very challenged during grief, producing a myriad of questions. They may have strong or negative reactions to God, like anger or disappointment. We state that it is our opinion that being angry or questioning God is very normal, and that God would welcome any of our feelings as we struggle. Further, people may well find themselves reworking their beliefs as a part of the growth of grief.

We welcome all responses as they struggle. Respectful of this, we take a neutral and accepting stance to any reaction, and trust God does, too.

Why We Do What We Do

A greater understanding of how we have made the program work is as follows:

- *Presenting a bulk of information up front*
  A great deal of grief information is given during the Foundations portions of the first three sessions. These basics provide a normalizing framework for participants' understanding of grief, and offer exercises for release and self-care training. Participants begin to recognize they have the ability to manage their own process, while allowing vulnerable feelings to pour forth. We use the image of the brain's ability to "make sense" of loss long before an emotional adjustment takes place. This same image can be applied to *Passages...through grief* overall. We appeal to the brain's function to learn new skills, and get to the issues and longings of the heart for healing.

- *Accepting new participants for Session Two*
  Often participants of *Passages...through grief* will attend Session One, and think about others they know who may benefit from the program. We, therefore, allow new participants to join Session Two. The group is closed after this to stabilize the group for trust building. See the "Session One Information for Leaders" for information about managing the entrance of new participants.

- *Participant's Attendance*
  From the beginning, participants' attendance is emphasized. The group is also told if a meeting must be missed, they are expected to notify the leader(s). When this happens, a time will be set to meet with the member so the material can be reviewed and the assignment can be clarified. This allows the participant to come to the next session prepared to actively participate. It has been found that a member can miss one session and make up that loss. However, when two or more sessions are missed, the suggestion is for the participant to repeat *Passages...through grief* at a later date.

- *Use of Yeagley's readings*
  You will find chapters of Larry Yeagley's book, *Grief Recovery*, at the end of each session. The book is no longer in print, but permission was given by Mr. Yeagley to use his materials in the *Passages...through grief* program. We have chosen his writings as they provide good information on grief from losses of many varieties, give guidance on how to intentionally grieve, and suggest resource tools to promote processing of grief. They are brief, manageable writings for the grieving reader. Since Mr. Yeagley is a retired minister, faith references are used throughout his

writings. Addressing spiritual matters is not a mission of **Passages...through grief**. See "Where is God in All This?" in Leader's Guide. It is not our intent to use Yeagley's writings to address faith issues but to provide another resource.

- ### Reading aloud to the group
  Core information about grief is read aloud by the leader. For example, we read the "Grief is..." articles. Many participants are struggling with the effects of grief on their concentration and focus. Hearing the words read aloud while they follow along in their manuals, allows for a greater absorption of the information. In addition, the leader's affect provides emphasis for key points.

- ### Beginning weekly assignments during the session
  When assignments are made, it sounds fairly easy to do the work at home. But it is not. Participants hesitate and may be unfocused on how to do the work. Beginning the work in session gives a "head start" or a point of reference from which to work when participants continue at home. It also provides the opportunity to ask questions or receive support as needed. We have found that participants are more likely to do the work when it is begun in session for just a few minutes.

- ### Using humor
  Grief is a heavy topic. During weekly sessions there is much to learn and many emotions are felt and shared. Using humor helps to lighten the heaviness and give the participants a moment of relief. In addition, it pulls the group participants together, teaches them that laughing is acceptable, and that laughter feels good! Of course, humor must be used appropriately by the leaders or facilitators, but it is a valuable part of the experience.

- ### Using rituals
  A number of rituals are used in the **Passages...through grief** sessions. Rituals are valuable and stabilizing tools that carry meaning and intentional focus. The use of the moment of silence to open each session, deep breathing exercises, and stating a feeling to close each week are all in place to give a sense of sharing, comfort, and control to participants. The "Letting Go" ritual in Session Five invites naming an issue, willingness to release, and a new frame of reference toward change. We suggest leaders make the rituals an effective part of the sessions by being habitual, calm, and deliberate as they offer them.

- ### Use of the moment of silence
  Following the welcome at the beginning of each session, the leader invites the participants to share in a moment of silence to "recognize their courage." This establishes to the participants, and reiterates for the leaders, that it takes courage to come to a group and be active in the grief process.

- ### Closing circle
  "Naming a feeling" in the closing circle for each session gives the participants a chance to voice a feeling and be heard. It also bonds their care for each other.

- *Charging a fee for the program*

  Generally, participants bring with them a hesitancy to participate in the program. They admit to the fear of the unknown. So, when participants pay a fee, they are more likely to make a personal commitment to complete the program and become invested in the process. The cost should be included in all advertising. The fee should be large enough to make it worthwhile to finish the six weeks. To establish the fees, consider cost of provisions, advertising, materials, payment of leaders and facilitators, and any other associated expenses. We have found it workable to offer weekly payments or partial scholarships to those with financial challenges.

- *Sharing a meal at the last session* (**Optional**)

  During the sessions the participants form a common bond, share their situations and feelings, and become emotionally close to each other through the work that is done. We take time at the final session to share a meal to give us social time together. It's an enjoyable event, allowing the participants to use their culinary skills (or show their skill in shopping to bring a store-bought item), have fun as a group, and celebrate the hard work that has been done. The final session should be scheduled to begin one half hour early to allow for the meal. The evaluation form should be introduced after the meal has been eaten, and completed prior to the work of the final session.

Sharing Groups

There are many skills that can be supported within the sharing groups. Hopefully, leaders and facilitators will have had their own group experiences or training, so that they can be cognizant of group dynamics and group process. In addition, there are numerous valuable resource texts to assist in understanding. This knowledge allows the facilitator to be proactive in guiding the group, while not taking charge of the process. If the leader recognizes their own lack of group background, we would encourage them to tap into the professional community for some supervision. Facilitating the sharing groups successfully is a mandate for *Passages...through grief*.

The ideal size for a sharing group is six to eight participants. If the whole group is not large enough for this division, it is fitting to keep the entire small-sized group together for sharing.

A major vehicle for healing within the program occurs in sharing groups. Fellow participants become sounding boards for each other, primarily offering listening, caring, and empathy. Grievers are tender for each other's pain. And so it is our goal as leaders to effectively use this rich resource, safe-guarding that participants are not overwhelmed. The emotional safety of the participants is key. If the participants within the sharing groups are able to deal with the weekly issues and evoked feelings of others, this is the preferred use of the group's time and energy.

Participants need skills to be effective group members. With clear guidance of how to "be in group," they learn to encourage others' sharing openly without judgment. They usually need to be guided away from advice-giving, comparing the gravity of losses, and asking too many directive questions. These skills can be modeled for them by the group facilitator. Learning to paraphrase the feeling statements of others will require gentle nudges.

When the groups are limited in their capacity to participate in the open-ended process discussed above, more direction will be required from the facilitator. There are a variety of circumstances that result in the "limitation of the group." For this reason, there is an expanded discussion of "Red Flags" for the leader to use. The weekly schedules for leaders include specific ideas for questioning or exploration that can make sharing group time productive.

The feedback we receive from participants completing *Passages...through grief* is that they most remember the people they met, referring specifically to fellow sharing group members with whom they bonded. Frequently, they will continue these relationships beyond the course of the program. We have heard years later of former participants who have kept up with each other and continue mutual support. This is a hallmark of a successful group experience. May you find this to be true for your participants.

Use of Reflection Time

Reflection time provides an intentional time to take thoughts and feelings that matter, and claim them through writing. It can be a valuable processing tool for those who are willing to use it. The writer learns that feelings can be recognized, claimed, and released. This gives the writer a sense of control in a very out of control time. "Reflection Time" pages have instructions to write after each weekly *Passages* session and the six days following.

Some participants will take to writing like a duck to water. These are generally the people who will work hard throughout the program, and feel a sense of accomplishment and release.

A few participants will fight with themselves and resist doing this work. It is almost as if they are afraid of what they might reveal to themselves. Others dislike writing. So writing one feeling word might be the first "small step."

Encourage the participants to use the writing tools listed in the "Reflection Time Guide." Additionally, you may want to emphasize the following to them:

- Dedicate themselves to the time, so writing can become a treasured experience.
- Find a safe place to keep their writings, like in the car or in a locked file cabinet.
- Use of a computer may be preferred over writing by hand. Use a flash drive can insure privacy.
- If a person refuses to write, suggest they talk out their thoughts, either to another person or into a recording device.

Deep Breathing and Guided Visualizations

During **Passages...through grief** use is made of deep breathing and guided visualizations for peaceful relaxation and personal grounding. The purpose is to demonstrate that participants can use these simple skills for self-support, and recognize a quiet meditative mood as another way to have control in their own grief process. Most people experience these strategies as a real benefit. A few will not like them, which is fine.

Both deep breathing and guided visualizations are initiated by asking people to sit comfortably in their chair with feet on the floor, close their eyes and take several slow, deep breaths. The leader uses a quiet, calm voice to give suggestions slowly and articulately. Participants are told to "imagine inhaling peace" and then "exhaling stress and strain." The remainder of the different activities vary according to the particular purpose for that session. Directions for these follow and are reiterated with separate session notes for the leader's guidance and convenience. If time allows, the group may want to use these quiet moments near the close of several sessions. Participants are also encouraged to use deep breathing meditation times at home. Some participants complain that their minds are inundated with thoughts while trying to be meditative. A suggestion may be made that they say to themselves, "Be quiet, chatter. I'll listen to you later."

In order to be effective, the leader's readiness to create a quiet and calm atmosphere is essential. It is suggested that the guided visualizations be practiced several times, so that they will be read smoothly and slowly, and with a quiet, neutral voice.

Deep Breathing (Session One)

Participants are asked to sit comfortably with their feet on the floor and close their eyes—gradually bringing their focus to the breaths they are taking. Suggest they allow their breathing to be normal and natural and just follow along. They can imagine they are inhaling "peace" and exhaling "stress and strain." The leader participates and allows the process to continue 3-5 minutes. At the conclusion, the group is told to let their attention come back to their body, and gradually open their eyes to the count of three. After a time, the leader may ask for feedback about the experience, reassuring that there is "no one right way." Encourage participants to try this practice for themselves at home, extending the breathing meditation 10 or 20 minutes.

Guided Visualization (Session Three)

Once relaxed and breathing calmly, participants are asked to imagine themselves in a quiet and peaceful place in nature (allow time.) Suggestions are made to gradually notice the sights, sounds, and smells of their surroundings. Then there are 1-2-3 minutes of silence.

When ready to conclude, the leader says, "You may return to this peaceful place any time you wish. And now you can come back to this room, little by little, and open your eyes to the count of three." Allow several moments for participants to complete their quiet time.

It may be helpful later to explain that they may remain solely with minutes of deep breathing. This can be particularly helpful when feeling stressed. The visualization, on the other hand, is more applicable when there is an unhurried period of time, say at their reflective writing time.

Leaders may find that their group responds well to these moments of quiet-taking and visualizations. If so, this process may well be used during other sessions, as well.

Guided Visualization (Session Five)

The latter part of Session Five is dedicated to a releasing ceremony. As this experience is meant to be solemn and meaningful, the participants are led through several steps toward release of an important feeling or situation. After a brief discussion of how difficult it is to let go and release, a sheet is handed out for participants to complete (use Session Five "Letting Go"). Subsequently, the release papers are collected in a basket and a guided visualization ensues. Once relaxed and breathing quietly, participants are asked to imagine themselves in a quiet and peaceful place in nature. Suggestions are made to gradually notice the sights, sounds, and smells of their surroundings. The text of the guided visualization follows:

PREPARATION:

"Relax, close your eyes, take 3 deep breaths inhaling peace and exhaling stress/strain."

READ SLOWLY:

"Go to a safe place in nature...sit and notice your surroundings...how peaceful this place is. // Gradually, you notice people who have loved you moving into your space...smiling at you. You stand in the center and they surround you. // Their arms are outstretched, offering love to you. Your heart is warmed. You thank them for the love you've been given. From them flow yarn fibers that are knit to create a colorful shawl that surrounds you... encircling you with care and warmth and reassurance. This is a shawl of healing for your spirit. Breath in deeply the calm...the love...the peace...the wholeness meant for you.// You can take this with you...you can take this with you as you quietly come back to this room. Slowly, you will notice the chair beneath you and gradually you will open your eyes...to experience this present moment."

Burn "Letting Go" sheets in crockery (lined with heavy foil) in silence.

Take care and offer hugs.

Program Guidelines

The program is open to adults, ages 18 and older.

The program is open to all types of loss.

Registration is necessary.

There is a fee for the series; scholarships may be made available.

There are six sessions in the program:

    Sessions One through Five are held for two hours.

    Session Six is two and ½ hours to provide time to share a meal.

It is helpful to find sponsors for the program such as churches, local colleges, individual counselors, counseling services, mental health programs, individuals, etc.

    Sponsors may provide support through:

        Advertising

        Making referrals

        Providing a location to have the program

        Providing refreshments

        Donating supplies

        Providing financial scholarship for participants

The group should accept new participants for Sessions One and Two only.

Passages...through grief Registration

Name

_____

Phone number(s)

_____

Address

_____

Email address

_____

Type of losses you have had _____

The registration fee is _____ Make check payable to_____

_____

To be completed by Leader:

Paid By: Cash_____   Check_____   Scholarship_____

Payment Form

Amount Due: _____

Name of Participant	Date Amount Paid Cash/Check	Date Amount Paid Cash/Check	Date Amount Paid Cash/Check	Date Amount Paid Cash/Check	Date Amount Paid Cash/Check

Provisions and Preparations for Weekly Sessions

- Room for large group sessions
    - Using a casual room with sofas and chairs is preferable
    - Place seating in a circle
- Additional room(s) for sharing group(s)
    - Place seating in a circle
- Tables for refreshments and registration
- List of registrants with space for notation of weekly payments
- Registration forms
- Manuals—one for each participant
- Nametags and markers
- Directional signs
- Posters for each session
- Pencils and pens
- Tissues for all meeting rooms
- Note cards (for questions participants want addressed)
- Ice water
- Cups
- Napkins
- Candy (hard candy, does chocolate make grief easier??!!)
- Small snacks may be offered
- Tape
- Masking tape
- Scissors
- Paper
- Extra "Reflection Time" sheets
- Weekly "Letters" to be sent to participants – one per person
    - o Envelopes
    - o Stamps
- For Session Three:
    - o A sample chart for "My Loss History"
    - o Thick rubber band for closing exercise

- For Session Four:
    - o Leader's story and chart – a brief personal review of a relationship that needed grieving to be read to the group as a preview to the exercise, "Charting the Relationship"
    - o A sample story and chart to use for development of Leader's own story
- For Session Five:
    - o Copies of "Letting go" sheets
    - o Pencils
    - o Small table
    - o Candle
    - o Basket for collecting completed sheets
    - o Lighter or matches
    - o Crockery to burn sheets (use aluminum foil in the bottom)

Posters for *Passages...through grief*

Posters need to be displayed around the room to highlight session points. You may use poster board, foam board, or anything of a large size. More than one poster may be required for each session. Any of these charts may be used throughout the program, as seems fitting for the group attending.

Posters are suggested for the following weeks

Sessions One through Six

One copy of the "Affirmation" poster is needed for each small group. Have the participants read the affirmation aloud together at the beginning of each small group time.

"I promise to keep confidential what others share, to be honest, and to respect my own unique grief journey."

Session One

Grief Changes Us

> Physically
> Emotionally
> Psychologically
> Socially
> Relationally
> Spiritually

For Sessions One - Three

Grief is...

> Normal
> Natural
> Process
> Difficult
> Active
> Self-centered
> Unique to You
> Result of a loss that mattered
> Has a beginning, a middle & an end

Session Two

Waves of Grief

Change in
Intensity
Frequency
Duration

Healing Wave (leader draws a wave to emphasize the movement of grief)

Factors Affecting Grief (from Yeagley's "Anatomy of Grief")

Manner of loss
Time to anticipate
Quality of relationship
Age/Health of griever
Beliefs/Attitudes
Support of others
Who we are when the loss occurs
Coping history
Permission from self to experience feelings & process

Sessions Two through Six

Definitions

Grief: The incompatible feelings resulting from a loss that mattered.
Process: The combination of experiences and feelings over time that is included in the grief journey.
Recovery: Recognizing and completing the unfinished business of the loss.

Grief has

a Beginning - feelings of loss are first felt
a Middle - time of processing
an End - the pain of the loss is not foremost

The timeline is unique to the griever, based on doing the necessary grief work.

Session Three

Healthy Adjustment:

    Our choice to get support
    Our need to share feelings
    Have feelings heard without judgment
    Resist being hurried

Session Four

Leader's Relationship Timeline

One leader should fill out a personal timeline to demonstrate how to complete the process.

HEALING = TIME + SMALL STEPS

Weekly Letters for Participants

A letter is sent to each participant after each of the six sessions. The letter is signed by the leaders, and is mailed immediately following the session in order to be received by the participants ASAP. The final letter may be mailed a week or two after the program concludes.

The letters reflect the information learned during the session meeting, gives statements of encouragement, and is a reminder of the assignments for the week. The participants have appreciated the receipt of the letters, saying they are a welcome reminder of the work they are doing, and that they are not alone in the process.

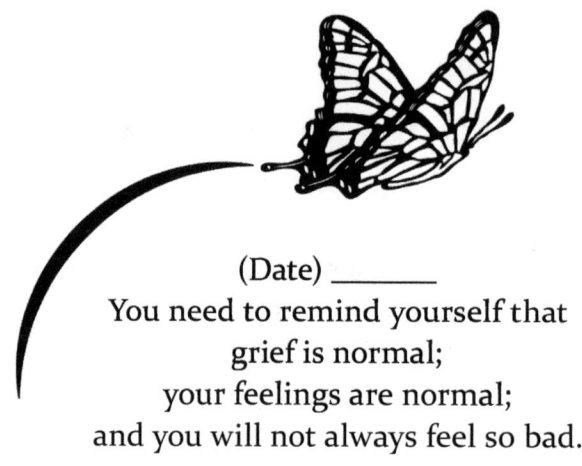

(Date) _____
You need to remind yourself that
grief is normal;
your feelings are normal;
and you will not always feel so bad.

Dear

We really appreciate the courage and honesty that you brought to **Passages...through grief.** It was not easy for you to come, we know. Hopefully, each session will provide insight to lead you to an understanding of your loss and a mellowing of your pain. What is happening to you is important, so we want you to have a safe place to talk and think about the challenges you are dealing with at this time.

Grief work is not easy, but we encourage you to try the assignments. Remember, to write and think and cry and talk is a **single task**, NOT four choices. Think of the goals of your grief recovery. Think of what you want for yourself.

Next week will be the last week for new people to join our group. If you know anyone who may be interested, please let them know. We look forward to seeing you next _____ -- same time, same place. If you have concerns or questions, please call _____(name) _____ (phone) or _____(name) _____(phone). We want to support you on your journey.

In the midst of all you are going through this week, may you know that you are cared for.

Grace and peace,

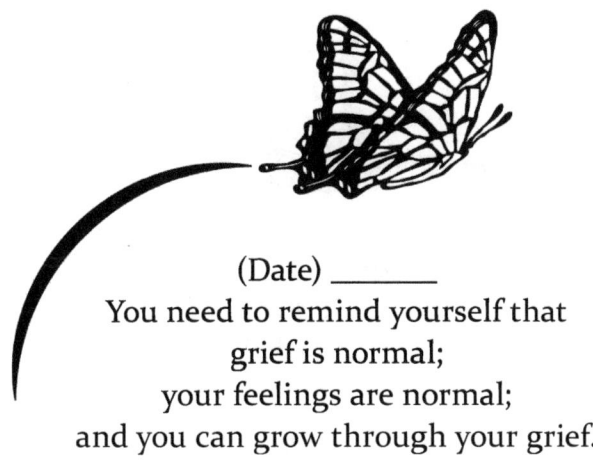

(Date) _____
You need to remind yourself that
grief is normal;
your feelings are normal;
and you can grow through your grief.

Dear

People usually need to express all sorts of feelings after the assignments of Session Two. Continue to **write and write**. This may raise pain and you may experience temporary depression, but the only way to a healthy understanding of your grief is through the pain itself. Please remember that no two people grieve alike and that it is helpful to share with others. We also gain insight when we listen to others.

For the next four sessions you will learn new information about grief that you can apply to your own situation. You will be given tools to help with your grieving process. You will also have time to ask questions related to your situation and share ideas and concerns with group members. We want you to feel you are in a safe place.

The present group is now closed; no new participants will be registered. We look forward to seeing you next _____

Grace and peace,

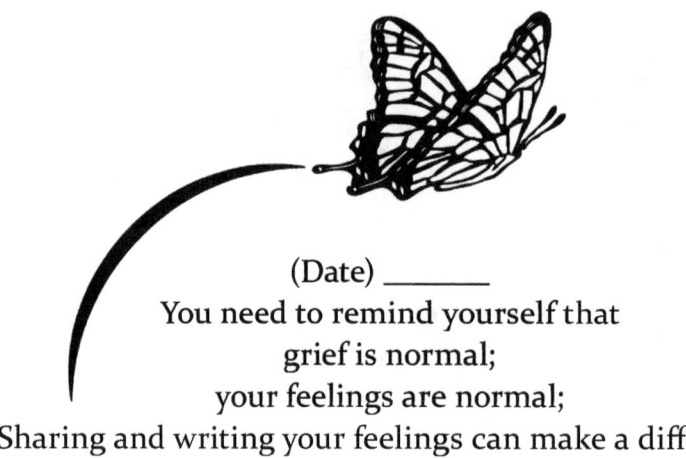

(Date) _____
You need to remind yourself that
grief is normal;
your feelings are normal;
Sharing and writing your feelings can make a difference.

Dear

    You have attended half of our program and you have gained skills to use with your own loss. When you are grieving, you are under stress. Tension builds up, muscles tighten, and you need to unwind. This can become a real problem. What helps you to relax? Try the stress relaxation exercises that are in the Yeagley readings and adopt some of the "self-care relievers of grief." Find out what is best for you. You are in charge of how you relax, how you deal with your stress.

    Start filling in your personal loss history graph, found at the end of the third session notes. You will need this for our next session. Also, keep a record of the questions you have for yourself, so you can begin to discover answers. We look forward to hearing your insights.

    Keep writing your "Reflections!" We look forward to seeing you next week.

Grace and peace,

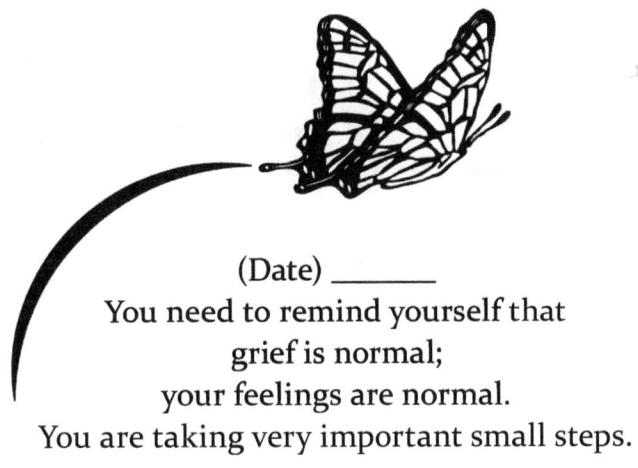

(Date) _____
You need to remind yourself that
grief is normal;
your feelings are normal.
You are taking very important small steps.

Dear

You probably have a fairly good list of questions for yourself regarding your grief process and your future. Hopefully you have begun to sort out some of your feelings. Remember, there are any number of "right ways" to deal with your grief. The main thing is to start. Choose what is helpful and set aside what is not.

Identifying feelings usually raises issues in terms of relationships. Making adjustments to all the new changes in your life, often raises other challenges. Everyone experiences new and unexpected difficulties when they grieve. Sometimes old issues or old pain resurfaces; sometimes relationships with people are strained. Have you tried ways to confront these? Are you discovering what is helpful for you and what is not? What are you doing to give yourself space to grieve and heal? Do you have a safe friend who will listen to you? Do you have someone who will listen to your relationship chart?

Remember to complete "Charting Our Relationship." Call if you have questions. Bring it along with your loss history chart next week. We'll go over this and develop how it can work for you next week. Keep on talking and writing (it's not too late to start!).

Also, please bring a memento to share with the other group members.

Grace and peace,

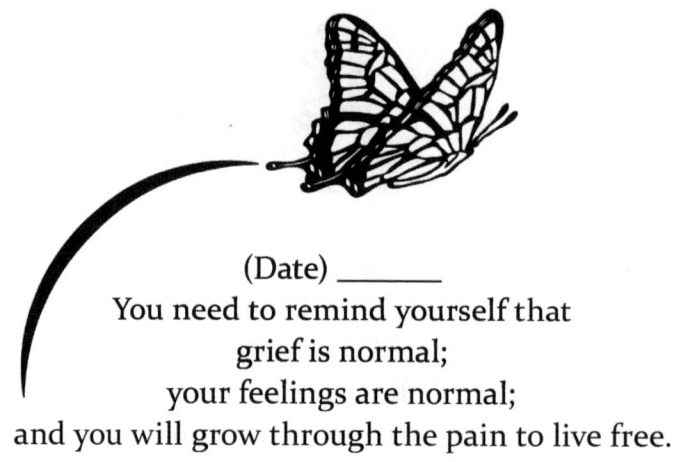

(Date) _____
You need to remind yourself that
grief is normal;
your feelings are normal;
and you will grow through the pain to live free.

Dear

So far we have covered many topics. Some may have been more challenging to you than others. We hope you have looked at some of the issues they cause you pain, for they are your vulnerable spots. Pain is healed by discovering the source and being open to healing.

Looking at your losses in life and confronting your own mortality are a part of the process. Discovering the incredible legacies given to you by people you've loved, helps you let go of what you no longer have, and helps you let go of the feelings which destroy your ability to live again with hope. You want to be able to reuse the love you have received. The assignments each week are the tools to help you work your way through your losses and discover new possibilities for living each day. Have you been "good to yourself" and to 'someone else' during the past week?

Please bring your *"Charting Our Relationship"* and *"My Letter of Declaration"* to our final session to be held next _____.

Grace and peace,

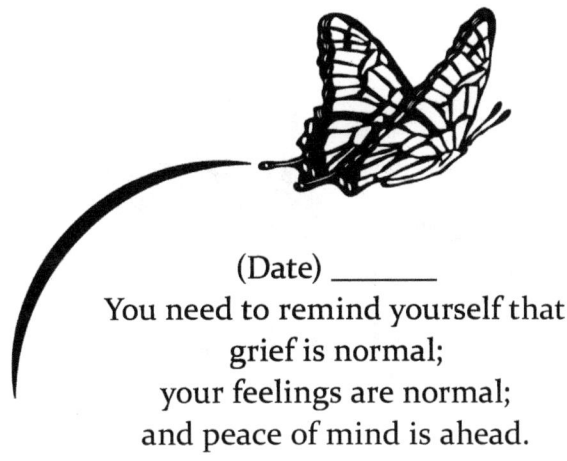

(Date) _____
You need to remind yourself that
grief is normal;
your feelings are normal;
and peace of mind is ahead.

Dear

    You have been in our thoughts these past few weeks, as you continue on your grief journey. Most people miss the weekly support of the group, and may feel somewhat lonely as they proceed on their own. However, we want to remind you that you carry with you the words of support and encouragement you heard from us and your sharing group. You also have a range of new skills to use as you take more "small steps" in completing the work you began. It may be helpful to review some of your exercises and writings to access the goals you had set, along with noticing the steps you took during the group sessions. The written materials are there for you to use. Now might be an important time to engage in more intentional grief work. The Yeagley writings are useful in that process.

    Hopefully, you found that "Reflection Time" during **Passages...through grief** was a valuable tool. Writing your thoughts and feelings will always be a positive option as you move along your own passage, and support the person you are growing to be.

Grace and peace,

Leaders:

Passages...through grief

A program for healing life's losses, such as death, divorce, relationship strain, health issues
Learn to understand and cope with grief, and bring hope to your life.

When: 6 sessions beginning _____

Time: _____

Where: _____

Cost: _____(scholarships available)

Leaders:_____

For more information and to register, please call

Sponsored by

Advertising Outlets

Newspaper advertisement or article

Church bulletins

Passages...through grief banner placed in a location easily seen

Flyers placed in public locations – examples:

- Libraries
- Churches

Emails/letters to:

- Hospitals
- Funeral homes
- Support groups – examples:
    - o Compassionate Friends
    - o Mental Health organizations
- Employee Assistance Programs
- Hospice organizations
- Pastoral Counseling Services
- Psychiatrists and Psychologists
- Clergy
- College chaplains and counselors

Sample of Announcements or Moments of Concern

Frequently public meetings or church services will allow for announcements to be made. The following are samples used in the past to capture attention and encourage people to consider grief work for themselves or others they know.

Sample

We are welcoming the full flowering of spring and signs of new life. However, there are those among us who are having a true burdensome time. Naturally, we think of loss first by death. But it could be a divorce or a broken relationship, loss of physical abilities, a career or a community. Life brings any number of difficult losses we need to grieve.

So often when people are experiencing grief, they think it is their lot...something they have to get through alone. They feel helpless to reach out for healing for any number of reasons, and settle for the dark cloud unresolved grief has left on their lives. For as we know, time alone does **not** heal wounds.

As a community we need to take a few moments today to recall those we know who have gone through losses...this year, last year or years ago. We can see some of their compromised living. Or we may find ourselves wondering how they are doing. Let us stop and care for them, and help them make it to the upcoming *Passages...through grief.* It begins _____. In the program we learn how the grief process works, share together and use exercises that help healing take place. It can make a difference in people's lives. Call _____ with questions and to register.

Sample

We are passing through the holidays, maybe feeling uncomfortable from the excesses. However, there are those among us who are having a true, burdensome time midst all the glitter and celebrations. We think of loss first by death. But it could be a divorce, loss of physical abilities, or a broken relationship.

So often when people are experiencing grief, they may think, "I have to get through this alone." They feel helpless to reach out for support for any number of reasons, and settle for the dark cloud unresolved grief has left on their lives.

As a community, we need to take a few moments today to recall those we know who have gone through losses...this year, last year, or further ago. We can see some of their compromised living. Or we may find ourselves wondering how they are doing. Can we stop, and care for them, and help them make it to the upcoming grief series, *Passages... through grief*? It begins on _____ and can make a difference in people's lives.

Evaluation Results

At the conclusion of each *Passages...through grief* series, we collect evaluations of the program. From these have come personal comments we have found inspiring and useful in promoting the program. Feel free to make use of the following quotes, as you collect your own.

- o "It is a very worthwhile experience, if you are willing to do the work. In fact, it can be life-changing."
- o "It was very helpful to be in the group with people going through different losses. We can all learn from each other's experiences."
- o "I am better for this experience."
- o "A wonderful program that is very useful to anyone faced with grief."
- o "I found it very interesting that I came to class so I could begin to grieve death, however, I found so many other things which I am making peace with."
- o "It's tremendously healing and helpful."
- o "I wish I had this information years ago. It would have made my life less painful."
- o "Useful in confronting difficult issues that you'd prefer to avoid. It forces you to push yourself – so you can progress through the grief process more deeply and fully and thus more healthily."
- o "It is a 'have to' following any deep loss."
- o "It was very, very helpful. I'm so blessed to have been here."

Responses to the question, "When I think of *Passages...through grief* I will remember..."

- • "How well structured and caring the group was. I absolutely loved it."
- • "That it was a way to spring board out of my grief and into a new me. I've got tools to tackle other changes in my life."
- • "My therapist is very grateful to you for helping me to deal with, and move past the grief that she and I have struggled with."
- • "That I was helped to move from my 'stuckness' and sadness very quickly."
- • "The true progress I made in 6 weeks, thanks to the guidance and support I received."
- • "Working through and finishing some of my most lingering griefs."
- • "Humor, tears, friendship and my ultimate ability to let go of some of the pain in me from the past."
- • "The ways to release grief, guilt, regret."

- "How helpful it was. How it gave my life back."
- "It was a good course … difficult… courageous…healing. It's all about the process. I hate the process."
- "It made me face the hurt of grief and begin to heal."
- "By working to continue to let go of my grief, long and short term, I have now been able to achieve a peace of mind that I have never known before."

Promoting *Passages...through grief*

There are numerous ways to promote the program and several are offered. You will certainly find your own ways to get the message out. First, in speaking directly with pastors, mental health professionals or small groups, an overview of the program is useful in informing and generating questions. Three different overviews of varying lengths are offered below, depending on the purpose or time-frame of the conversation.

Passages Overview

Passages...through grief is a six-week series for changing the way we see grief.

We learn

> Grief is a <u>process</u>
> How to understand grief
> How to intentionally grieve
> How to cope with the life changes and bring to hope

We experience

- Different types of loss (e.g., death, divorce, jobs, health) share similarities in the grief process
- Various aspects of grief are made personal
- Support and structure for healing current and unresolved losses
- Value of sharing loss and feelings within a safe group
- Difficult feelings like guilt, anger, and forgiveness can be resolved

Passages Session Schedule

- Foundations (1 hour)
  Learning how grief works and how to heal
- Sharing groups (45 minutes)
  Personal sharing
- Weekly assignments
  Written projects to personalize learnings
  Reflective exercises to work through grief

Focus of Session Activities

- **Session One**: get oriented and develop goals; personal contract to work; begin "Grief is..." and sharing groups
- **Session Two**: the erratic "waves" of grief's pain; depression scale
- **Session Three**: healthy vs. unhealthy grief relievers; stress test; loss history graph (variety of losses across the years)
- **Session Four**: dealing with hard feelings, using "Charting Our Relationship" (in-depth review of one relationship)
- **Session Five**: use of "My Letter of Declaration" for unfinished words; forgiveness—what it is not, how to begin
- **Session Six:** sharing a meal, feedback, and declaration letter; recognition of learnings; repeat depression scale (note changes); good-byes

Passages Quick Overview

- Grief as process—supporting courage and personal written commitment; recognizing grief myths and forbidden clichés others use (that don't help)
- Kinds of losses and why we grieve the way we do; the effects of holidays and anniversaries and how to "make it through"
- Focus on difficult feelings (like anger and guilt); forgiveness and letting go with intentional grieving
- Use of readings, small group sharing, and reflective writing to facilitate the healing process

Passages Overview Statement

The ***Passages...through grief*** program is unique, in that it provides a group experience for those having all types of losses. We have found that the type of loss is not as significant as the responses to grief, which are similar. The combination of a variety of losses enables the leaders and participants to publicly recognize that loss, in any form, has power. Respect for the loss is demonstrated by an accepting, nonjudgmental attitude where no comparisons of losses are made by leaders or participants, alike.

Passages...through grief is a six-week series for changing the way we see grief, and addresses issues in a systematic and practical way. By coming to understand how grief operates, participants are encouraged to work through the feelings of grief, to develop skills to use in the process, and to complete the incompleteness of their loss. In addition, those who are active in partaking of the program's educational component, find there is assistance in understanding grief and healing overall. They come to recognize how the process works through their thoughts, feelings, and relationships. Progressively, they are supported in efforts to process through the varied aspects of their personal grief journey.

Unresolved Grief

When speaking with people about the benefits of *Passages...through grief,* it is valuable to make reference to unresolved grief. This expands the list of potential participants to those whose losses have not been healed, or whose lives are in turmoil, or depression.

The following statements and illustrations may be useful in spurring the listener's attention:

The fear of being overwhelmed by grief is PARADOXICAL:
By avoiding grief, we are overwhelmed—blocked from the life available to us.
By pushing down the things "we wish we'd said or done," we are held captive by regrets, resentments, guilt, etc.

Two men at church cried last week...
One lost his wife, the other his son. Their grief is still active after more than twenty months. Society understands physical treatment and healing, NOT emotional. Society does NOT know how to encourage the healing of grief.

Grief is a wound:
What's required to heal the wound? Clean and tend the hurt + time
What happens if it's not treated and we slap on a band aid? Infection / compromised physical and emotional health

What areas are affected by unresolved grief?
Physical
Spiritual
Emotional
Psychological
Relational
Social

Stories for emphasis of unresolved grief:

1. The blocked grief of Brendan

A car accident (sudden, shocking) caused the deaths of his mom and sister. The sister's children needed Brendan's attention, so his grief was put off. He can't speak of the loss without tearing up, experiencing anxiety, headaches, and stomach problems. Brendan's comments about loss: "It's like it happened yesterday." "I feel so guilty...I lived, sis died, and missed her life." "Dad's been lost without mom and cheated by God." These losses have framed Brendan's life. Areas impacted: emotional, physical, relational, spiritual, lost perspective and memories (stuck back at the accident).

2. Numbed grief of Jake & Sarah

The couple lost their 4-year-old child to leukemia. Rather than clinging to each other and letting grief "own them for a while," they were terrified by fears of "losing it." Consequently, they retreated from grief and each other: Jake to drinking; Sarah to crafts and church volunteering. Their gradual inability to talk about their lost child produced more silence and pulled them apart as a couple. They became strangers, awkward together. Their numbed, harbored, silenced grief evolved into resentment and apathy—limiting life AND their ability to treasure the memories of the lovely and challenging moments/years of life together with their child.

Session One

Session One Information for Leaders

Corresponding Participant's Manual (PM) page numbers are noted in parenthesis. For example, p. 59 (PM p. 3) means Leader's Guide page 59 and Participant's Manual page 3 offer the same material.

Passages Foundations (45-50 minutes)

Welcome
Leader introduces a moment of silence to recognize their courage in coming

- Refer to **Why We Do What We Do** p. 18

Provide housekeeping information:

- Location of bathrooms
- Meeting time and the importance of being on time
- Number of weeks in program
- Available refreshments and tissues
- Invite questions of leaders by using notecards (provided)
- Silence cell phones

Group Contract for *Passages...through grief* p. 59 (PM p. 3)

- Read aloud and have each participant sign

Introduction of leaders and facilitators

- Name
- Credentials
- Loss history
- What brought them to lead *Passages...through grief*

Introduction of group members—stress brevity

- Name
- Loss that brings them to the program

Review **Recognizing Losses** p. 60 (PM p. 4) - Emphasize variety
Review and discuss **Myths and Realities of Grief** p. 62 (PM p. 6)

- Refer to **What Society Says about Grieving** p. 9
- Ask participants about their own myths

Review and discuss **Grief is a Process** p. 63 (PM p. 7)

- Refer to **Doing Grief Work** p. 10

Read aloud **Small Steps** p. 65 (PM p. 9)

- Clarify understanding
- Refer to **Taking Control** p. 12
- Have participants begin the activity (use about 5-10 min.)

Break (5 – 10 minutes)

Leaders use this time to define sharing group membership as outlined in **Leadership Requirements** p. 2
At end of break, each facilitator gathers their sharing group members and moves to their meeting space

- Facilitators take the **Affirmation** poster p. 32

Sharing Group(s) (45 minutes)

In preparation, leader's refer to **Sharing Groups** p. 21
Read aloud together **Affirmation**
Ask participants to describe their personal loss experience
Ask, "Have you heard something tonight that makes you feel less alone or more 'normal'?"

In Closing (15 minutes)

Present assignment: **Responses to Grief** p. 66 (PM p. 10)
Review and discuss **Reflection Time Guide** p. 67 (PM p. 11)

- Use of Reflection Time p. 22

Review **Follow-up for the Week** (content page)

Announce that new members will be allowed in Session Two but not thereafter

Lead **Deep Breathing** for 3 - 5 minutes p. 57

- Refer to **Deep Breathing and Guided Visualizations** p. 23
- Remind participants they have a copy of **Deep Breathing** for their use (PM p. 14)

Closing Ritual—gather participants into a circle and invite them to, "Name a feeling you've felt tonight." To create a quiet and accepting atmosphere, leaders and facilitators invite participants to join hands and close eyes.

- One leader begins by stating a feeling
- Allow for silence
- Do not expect everyone to participate
- Conclude after appropriate length of silence for sharing by saying, "Go in peace."

Post Session Meeting for Leaders and Facilitators

Review and discuss:

- Progress or difficulties of individual participants
  - o Note referrals or other services needed
- The overall functioning of the whole group
- The overall functioning of the sharing group(s)
- Boundaries and responses to behaviors that detract from a healthy group (e.g., the excessive talking individual)
- Challenging responses to situations (e.g., comparing losses, person who doesn't share, very tearful person) that need addressing with the participant prior to the next session
  - o Who will address participant
- Prepare weekly letters for each participant
  - o Arrange for mailing

Provide support for each other!

Deep Breathing

(Leader Instructions)

Participants are asked to sit comfortably with their feet on the floor and to close their eyes...gradually bringing their focus to the breaths they are taking. Suggest they allow their breathing to be normal and natural and just follow along. They can imagine they are inhaling "peace" and exhaling "stress and strain." The leader participates and allows the process to continue 3-5 minutes. At the conclusion, the group is told to let their attention come back to their body and gradually open their eyes to the count of three. After a time, the leader may ask for feedback about the experience, reassuring that there is "no one right way." Encourage participants to try this practice for themselves at home.

Session One Guide for Participants

Follow-up for the Week:

Complete *Responses to Grief*
Review *Small Steps*
Read Yeagley's articles
    "Loss—The Broad Spectrum"
    "Coming—Ready or Not"
Use *Reflection Time* notes to support your writing for the week

Group Contract for
Passages...through grief

1. All group members are grievers.
2. Grief experiences are not to be compared. Each person here has his/her unique experience that is to be respected.
3. Confidentiality is a requirement of each group member. No one is to share the experiences or feelings of others outside of this group.
4. Open honesty and taking responsibility for dealing with your own grief issues is expected.
5. Sharing with others in the group is vital to your progress.
6. Be respectful in listening and allowing each member to have time to share in the group.
7. You may "pass" if you feel unable to share openly or respond at any point.
8. Attendance is a priority to making progress. Please notify a facilitator or leader if you must be absent.
9. If you wish to contact a group member, please ask that person for their information. The group leaders do not supply contact information.

Signature: _____

Date: _____

Recognizing Losses

There are many types of losses that evoke grief, though our society often fails to recognize the need for active grieving.

The variety of losses may include:

- The death of someone important to you
  - o Natural causes
  - o Accident
  - o Suicide
- A broken relationship
  - o Separation from a family member or friend
  - o Divorce
  - o Disillusionment or disappointment in a changed relationship
- Major job changes
  - o Losing a job
  - o Early retirement (forced)
- Loss of dreams, goals and aspirations; loss of sense of self
- Move, change in community of support or culture important to you
- Loss of community/personal relationships due to an acknowledgement of sexual identity
- Personal physical changes
  - o Chronic or life-threatening illness
  - o Suffering a disabling or disfiguring accident
- Dealing with physical, mental, or emotional changes of someone close to you
  - o Life-threatening illness
  - o Imminent death
  - o Ravages of dementia
  - o Placement in a nursing facility
  - o Serving in the care giving role – either physically or emotionally
  - o Menopause
- Judicial challenges
  - o Committing a felony
  - o Incarceration

- Pregnancy/newborn loss
  - o Miscarriage
  - o Termination
  - o Placement of baby for adoption
- Being attacked or violated physically or mentally
- Substance addiction or mental illness
- Being effected by natural disasters or acts of war
- Loss of special family pet

Myths and Realities About Grief

The Myth	The Reality
Grief is only meant for death.	We need to grieve ALL losses.
Grief is only felt by the immediate family.	Anyone affected by the loss has a need to grieve.
Grief is only emotional.	Grief is felt emotionally, physically, spiritually and mentally. Grief is the hardest work you will ever do.
Grief should be expressed in private.	We cannot always control where or when we grieve.
Grievers should be left alone.	Support is necessary for those grieving. Grievers need people who will care, listen and share in the memories without judgment.
Grief is felt in stages.	Grief is an irregular process with no set time frame. It is experienced in "waves."
Time heals all wounds.	Time is necessary but not sufficient. The best healer of pain is to process the feelings of loss. There is no set time frame for grief.
When you grieve you let go of the person or situation lost.	The need is to let go of the pain of the loss; then valuable memories can be kept.
Those who have a strong belief in God, or a higher being, have an easier time with loss.	Our beliefs may be questioned at a time of loss. Those who are strong believers still have to experience grief. Belief is no substitute for the pain of grief.

During *Passages...through grief*, you will learn

Grief is a process.

This process is different *for each person* <u>depending on</u>:

1. The relationship with the person or situation that is lost. This will be unique for you. Each loss you experience will be different because each relationship you have had is different.
2. The type of loss
3. How you have dealt with changes and losses in your past
4. How you have been taught through family experiences to deal or not deal with loss
5. Knowing that unresolved grief will negatively impact your life
6. Your willingness to allow the uncomfortable feelings (ex. pain, loneliness)
7. Your willingness to use physical and emotional energy to deal with the loss at this time
8. Your belief about...
   - The ability to heal
   - Faith or spiritual assurances
   - How others view this loss
   - How others will support your grieving
9. Your courage to reach out and ask for understanding, support, and assistance with those "things" you are not able to do alone

Where's God in All This?

Frequently grief groups and programs put a loud emphasis on religious beliefs and practices. We in *Passages...through grief* take a different stance.

It is our experience that grievers' reactions to 'God' references vary, even among 'believers', during the grief process. Those who find their faith strengthened tend to speak openly in the group about that reaction, about how much stronger their faith has grown during grief. Periodically, one of these folks may ask why we do not have prayer together. Acknowledging their faith experience, we explain that for some people faith is very challenged during grief, producing a myriad of questions. Grievers may have strong emotional reactions to God, like anger or disappointment. It is our opinion that being angry or questioning God is very normal, and that God would welcome any of our feelings as we struggle. Further, some people may well find themselves reworking their beliefs as a part of the growth of grief.

We welcome all responses as grievers struggle. In respect for this, we take a neutral and accepting stance to any reaction. And trust God does, too.

Small Steps...

**There are some big issues to be worked through while grieving.
Breaking them into Small Steps makes them workable and attainable.
They are**

- To accept that my loss is real
- To understand grief is a normal, necessary process
- To understand grief and the effect it has on my life
- To share feelings and experiences with safe, non-judgmental people
- To recognize strengths that I bring to the grief process
- To develop skills that will help me grow through grief
- To find a new normal for myself
- To take small steps

Small Step I will Take:	Result – feeling:
Examples: 1. I will ask for help with a task. 2. I will take ___ minutes each day to write about my feelings, etc.	Examples: 1. Reassurance that it is okay to ask. 2. I can identify and describe my feelings.

Responses to Grief

Check all responses that you have had from your current and former losses.

Emotional Responses	Current Loss	Past Loss
Relief		
Shock		
Sadness		
Fear		
Loss of control		
Abandonment		
Anger		
Freedom		
Yearning		
Loneliness		
Frustration		
Numbness		
Guilt/self-reproach		
Anxiety, excessive worry		
Helplessness		
Confusion		
Physical Responses		
Restlessness		
Appetite Changes		
Tightness in the chest or throat		
Increased number of illnesses		
Hollowness in stomach		
Oversensitive to noise		
Gastro-intestinal changes		
Weakness in muscles		
Heart palpitations		
Breathing disturbances		
Dry mouth		
Sense that nothing seems real		
Lack of energy		
Changes in activity level		
Sleep disturbances		

Behavioral Responses	Current Loss	Past Loss
Calling out for lost one		
Absent-mindedness		
Treasuring objects associated with loss		
Inability to maintain normal routine		
Taking on mannerisms of person who is gone		
Social withdrawal		
Experiencing physical ailments of persons who have died		
Seeing or hearing people when not present		
Fantasizing to explain what happened		
Appetite changes		
Avoidance of people/crowds		
Deep sighing		
Unexpected crying		
Loss of sexual desire		
Avoidance of certain places		
Over-activity		
Need to stay busy		
Underactivity/ lethargy		
Thought Responses		
Disbelief		
Dreams of the person		
Preoccupation with loss		
Inability to concentrate		
Sense of going "crazy"		
Slow reaction times		
Trouble remembering		
Difficulty making decisions		

Adapted from "Grief Counseling Grief Therapy" by J.W. Worden and "Bereavement" by C.M. Parkes

Reflection Time Guide

For the course of *Passages...through grief*, you are asked to dedicate time each day to reflect on:

- Feelings brought about by daily events
- Difficult emotional experiences (i.e., feeling helpless, angry, lonely)
- Your responses to our *Passages...through grief* sessions and discussions
- Special challenging days and events
- Changes in yourself, either positive or of concern to you

You have been given sheets entitled **Reflection Time** (XX) to use to record your thoughts and feelings. The recording of these allows you to gain a **sense of control** in what can be a very out-of-control-time in your life. It will also lead you to understand what is happening to you, when it may not be easily understood. And it will allow you to release or retain your feelings based on their importance or benefit.

Reflection time writing is a learned behavior. It can be difficult in the beginning but may be made easier by following the suggestions that are workable for you:

- Write for you and you only.
- Plan to keep your writing in a safe place so that sharing it with others is by your choice.
- If you are more comfortable using a computer, do so. You may wish to use a flash drive to insure privacy.
- Do not judge yourself on the feelings that come forward through your reflection and writing.
- Do not think about how anyone else would respond to your feelings.
- Do not attend to the details of proper grammar or punctuation, as doing so will restrict the flow of feelings and thoughts. Just write!!
- Be totally honest about your thoughts and feelings. Do not limit them in any way while writing; they cannot harm or offend others in **your** private space.
- Aim to write about the same time each day to encourage having reflection time become a habit.
- If you become stuck, leave it for a while and return when you feel able.
- Date each entry.
- Keep your writing to review and do not throw it away. It will be a good reference for you to see the progress you are making in your grief.

- Make this time special – a time just for you.
  - o Sit in a comfortable, private place
  - o Wear a prayer shawl, special robe, or a throw around your shoulders – something that brings you comfort
  - o Light a candle
  - o Play background music (optional)
- Writing can evoke much emotion—drink plenty of water to hydrate your body.
- A specific "Reflection Time" page is provided for use after each session. You are encouraged to complete it right after the session, if possible.
- A "Reflection Time" page is provided for each day to lead you to address certain feelings and thoughts, which will be necessary for the *Passages...through grief* program.

Oftentimes, during grief, it is difficult to name our emotional reactions. The **Feelings Chart** may be beneficial in helping you identify the various feelings you are experiencing.

Feelings Chart

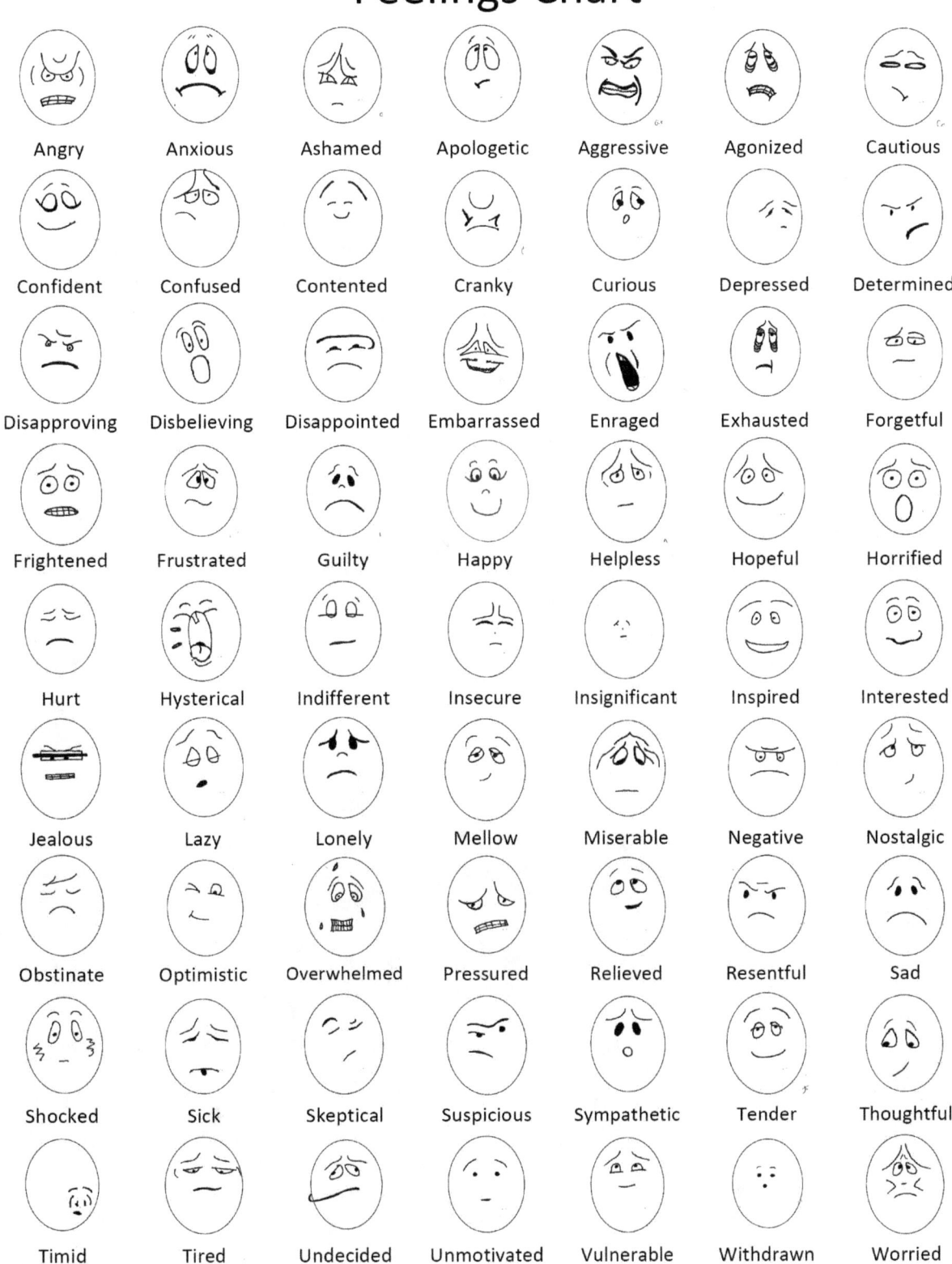

Angry	Anxious	Ashamed	Apologetic	Aggressive	Agonized	Cautious
Confident	Confused	Contented	Cranky	Curious	Depressed	Determined
Disapproving	Disbelieving	Disappointed	Embarrassed	Enraged	Exhausted	Forgetful
Frightened	Frustrated	Guilty	Happy	Helpless	Hopeful	Horrified
Hurt	Hysterical	Indifferent	Insecure	Insignificant	Inspired	Interested
Jealous	Lazy	Lonely	Mellow	Miserable	Negative	Nostalgic
Obstinate	Optimistic	Overwhelmed	Pressured	Relieved	Resentful	Sad
Shocked	Sick	Skeptical	Suspicious	Sympathetic	Tender	Thoughtful
Timid	Tired	Undecided	Unmotivated	Vulnerable	Withdrawn	Worried

Produced by Susan Williams, C-GC and Mary Ann Lippincott, Ph.D.

Deep Breathing

Sit comfortably in a chair with your feet on the floor and allow your eyes to close. Gradually bring your focus to the breaths you are taking. Allow your breathing to be normal and natural and just follow along. Imagine you are inhaling 'peace' and exhaling 'stress and strain.' Continue in this way for several minutes. When you are finished, gradually open your eyes to the count of three and recognize the present moment.

Yeagley's

"Loss—The Broad Spectrum"

Writing about loss reminds me of an old farmer who was admitted to the hospital for surgery. He had never been hospitalized before. As he talked about the limitations the physician was setting, he said, "I just don't know how I can part with her, but the doc says she's just too much for me to take care of." Tears were on the old man's face.

My heart went out to him, thinking that he was being forced to place his invalid wife in a long-term care facility. I carefully questioned him about the circumstances and soon discovered that his nearly 500-pound sow had to be sold. The pig's care required lifting heavy buckets and bending over the side of the pen. He could no longer do this. Saying goodbye to the old porker was a major loss.

"You may think I'm a fool to cry over an animal like this," he apologized, "but I've had her for a long time."

The pig was an important part of the farmer's support system. His grief was genuine and to be expected.

Most parents can relate stories about their children and the death of their pets. Real trauma is involved and real grief results.

My granddaughters were two and five when they moved into their new house in the country. Some cold-hearted person dropped three kittens off at the end of their lane. Two of them were claimed by Erin and Jamie. They called to seek my opinion on names for them. They invested hours into caring for their new friends.

Shortly after adopting the kittens they went to visit their friends in Kansas City. During the night a large German shepherd dog snatched away one of the kittens that managed to crawl out of the garage.

When the girls came home their hearts were broken. For days they carried cat food into the woods and called their kitten's name, but their friend never heard their call.

A couple months after they lost their kitten I visited them. We walked into the woods to search for birds and wildflowers. My job was to record what we saw. We sat on a big log and talked about our discoveries, but the conversation soon turned to the loss of their friend. I could hear the sadness in their little voices.

Loss begins the moment we are born. We lose that warm place beneath mother's heart where we are fed umbilically and rocked amniotically. We emerge into the world of light where we cry to get our food and rocking.

In childhood we lose being at home with parents all day long. Sometimes we are awakened early in the morning and driven to a creepy daycare center where we stand a chance of having little physical contact with a caring person for eight hours.

I stood outside a large church in St. Paul, MN, waiting for the pastor to open the room where I was to present a seminar. Next to the church was a daycare center. I watched dozens of parents delivering their babies and tiny tots to the center. Nearly every child screamed fearfully and clutched at their parent's body and clothes. Their separation anxiety still makes me sad when I drive past daycare centers.

Teenagers lose their identity. They are no longer children, but they are not yet adults. They want to be independent, but they still depend on warm meals and a clean bed to sleep in. They are on an emotional rollercoaster. In their quest for social togetherness they lose many boyfriends and girlfriends. Some of them have been pushed prematurely into dating and have lost their childhood.

People in their twenties lose their parental home. They no longer are foot-loose-and-fancy-free. They have to work to pay the apartment rent.

The middle years come quickly. All the big dreams and achievements are not half realized, but life is more than half over. Loss of dream can be upsetting.

In later years physical and mental deficits appear. Thinking fast and moving fast isn't easy. The chronic diseases of age take their toll.

There are at least three kinds of losses – maturational, situational and accidental.

Maturational loss is felt by the four-year-old when mother brings the new baby home from the hospital. It is sometimes referred to as having your nose out of joint, but to the four-year-old it seems as though the whole body is out of joint.

This is felt by the young bride leaving her parental home. I took my new bride to a honeymoon cabin on the Chesapeake Bay. On the first morning of our marriage I fixed the breakfast. When I called, "Come and get it," there was no response. I went to the bedroom and found her weeping on her pillow. She realized that marriage meant leaving her parental home. Homesickness had descended upon her – grief, if you please.

Maturational loss is not a static experience, it's more of a process. The new bride says goodbye to her parental home when she is old enough to marry. This is followed by losses such as having her own children leave home, selling the big family-sized house, and moving into a one-bedroom apartment designed for "senior citizens." It also includes losses such as the death of a parent or spouse, handicaps due to aging or the inability to drive an automobile.

Situational losses include such things as giving up a pet because of moving to a smaller place in the city, business failure due to economic recession, being fired from a job, and being laid off from work.

Sometimes situational losses are accompanied by secondary losses. For instance, a young man is fired from his job. He learns his lesson and vows to mend his ways on the next job, but due to low seniority, he is laid off from the new job when production slows down. His secondary loss is the shattering of his self-esteem which causes depression to set in.

Accidental losses include things like the sudden and tragic death of a loved one, loss of a limb or bodily function due to a mishap, or the destruction of a home in a tornado.

Losses of all types have a tendency to immobilize the loser, for a short time at least, because the losses do not fit into our scheme of life. Loss is contrary to our expectations.

The divorced people who attend grief support seminars often tell me that they grew up with a dream that they would meet an ideal person for a life companion and that they would always be in love. They pictured their spouses as faithful and totally fulfilled in the marriage. Then one day the horrible story is related – a story of broken vows and shattered dreams.

Divorce doesn't have a place in their expectations. They use denial tactics and entertain false hopes. A lot of energy is spent scheming ways to bring about a reconciliation beyond the point of reason. The loss of a spouse goes against everything they learned to be right and noble.

For some divorced people the word "single" sends chills up and down their spine. They use the word scores of times when referring to others, but they can't handle the use of the word when referring to themselves.

By the time some people attend a support group they have been to a half-dozen counselors looking for somebody to give them a magic formula for mending broken relationships. They may have consumed bottles of tranquilizers and lost many pounds or gained weight from the escape mechanism called "eating," all because their loss was shaped differently than the pattern of life's expectations.

Loss through divorce is devastating, particularly when a person says, "There's something wrong with me. I'm unlovely and incapable of wooing and keeping a mate. I'm doomed to spend the rest of my life alone. Even if somebody else came along I could never trust another person that much again."

Loss seems to inundate those who have no concrete plans for their lives. I heard one person say that everyone needs to have a plan that outlasts life expectancy. Then they need to become excited about the plan and work toward its accomplishment. Without such a plan, a person can be stopped in his tracks when loss occurs.

Another factor that makes loss so overpowering is the absence of a broad support system. People who isolate themselves and form few close friendships have little encouragement in times of loss.

If I'm swimming in deep water I make sure others are swimming with me. My chances of being brought to shore when I lose my endurance are a lot better. I go one step further by making sure I'm among good, strong swimmers.

Loss is an inevitable part of this life. It makes good sense to build into life the kinds of strengths and defenses that maximize the chances of turning losses into gains.

I met a woman who turned her losses into assets. She was a permanent resident of a county home. I was a neophyte pastor with a bundle of "promise texts" in memory to share with unfortunate people like Mabel.

The charge nurse called up to see if she was ready for company. The answer came back on the intercom - "Eager."

"Oh, I'm so happy you came to see me," she exclaimed. "I've been so eager to show off my beautiful roses. They just put this paper on the walls. I think the roses are absolutely exquisite. With the sun streaming in the windows they make my room look like a rose garden."

I didn't notice the roses on her wall paper. I was distracted by Mabel's blinded eyes. The diabetes had taken its toll.

"You'll never know how much it means to me to be in this home," she continued. "Do you know, there are some folks in this place who are too depressed for words. Why, if it wasn't for me they'd have no hope at all. I go around to their rooms every day and cheer them up."

My eyes followed the contour of her body beneath the covers. Just below the hips the covers were flat against the mattress. Mabel had no legs.

The nurse told me that the aides put Mabel in a special chair every day and wheeled her to all the wards. She was known as the angel of the county home.

This inexperienced pastor felt like a pygmy in the presence of a spiritual giant. In spite of her monumental losses, Mabel's assets rose above them.

I'm still trying to discover her secrets. It may be that the discovery can only be made in the presence of loss, but I suspect that Mabel's discovery was integrated into her life long before she went to the county home.

The broad spectrum of loss is not complete until we explore the secondary or abstract losses that are associated with primary losses. Identifying and experiencing these losses fully during acute grief reduces the chances of complicated grief.

Sometimes secondary losses are called psychological losses. An example is the man who was married to a talented musician. When he attended concerts where she performed, he experienced a great boost to his esteem. After the divorce he no longer experienced that regular boost. Eventually he disliked himself and lost confidence in his ability to form new relationships.

Loss of reputation was a secondary loss for a man who lost his freedom after a fraudulent business deal.

Loss of accomplishment was a secondary loss for a man who retired from his job.

Whether loss is primary or secondary, it can be triggered by many kinds of loss experiences. No loss should be minimized. All loss causes pain.

Yeagley's

"Coming—Ready or Not"

"I don't care how long you know in advance, you're just not ready for it when it happens."

"It hurts even though I had time to do a lot of things I wanted to do."

"She lived a long life and she had a lot of pain. I guess I should be thankful she's at rest, but I hate like everything to say goodbye."

"We both knew it couldn't be much longer. The doctor told us exactly what it was. We talked about it a lot, but I didn't think it would be today."

These are just a few statements I have heard people make right after the death of a loved one.

A business executive at a pre-retirement seminar asked, "Are you ever ready for the death of a person who is very important to you?"

The answer is probably "not completely." The reality is that death is much like the game of "hide and seek" – coming, ready or not.

When people are having a rewarding relationship together, they naturally reach toward the ever fuller development of life's potential. This seems to be a quality that was created into the human race. It was the Creator's plan that people should live forever – continually broadening and enriching every dimension of life.

Death is an enemy that has temporarily interrupted the plan. Despite the reality of death in this life, people usually plan for more living than they can squeeze into their days.

As one man put it who knew his wife was dying, "When the doc told us that Mary had six to nine months to live, we decided right then and there that we'd put six to nine years of living into those six to nine months."

We may not ever be completely ready for a death, but there are some simple concepts that make adjustment much easier when we practice them. Let me share them with you.

1. Let the people you love know who you are.

A man came to see me because he couldn't "get over" his wife's death. As he fought back the tears he said, "I never really showed my feelings to her. She never really knew me. I guess I was very quiet. Oh, she tried to get me to tell her my deep thoughts, but it's always been difficult for me to talk much."

Telling another person who you are is not as easy as it sounds.

I remember reading an article that suggested that when newlyweds fully undress in each other's presence for the first time, it is a pledge that they will be transparent and allow themselves to be seen without masking.

Undressing is child's play compared to the monumental task of self-revelation, yet letting loved ones know you is vital when it comes to adjustment after death.

Heart-to-heart talks about mutual interests, joys and sorrows can become a regular part of family life. There is no reason why philosophies of life, feelings about pain, sickness and death, and personal preferences about being informed of one's own illness and imminent death cannot be discussed openly.

This openness about every aspect of life will eliminate the game playing and "conspiracy of silence" that occurs during crises in far too many families.

A friend of mine asked me if I could take the time to drive to a distant city to see her parents. Her mother was in the hospital recuperating from a surgical procedure that revealed inoperable cancer. I was to visit with the couple at the hospital.

When I went to the hospital room it was meal time. The husband, I'll call him Jim, had gone to the cafeteria to get a bite to eat. I went to find him, but he wasn't eating. He was sitting in a small lounge in a quiet part of the hospital. After introductions I moved into painful territory.

"Jim, have you and Letha talked about cancer, treatments or the chances of her death?" I asked.

"Not very much," he said with a sigh. "I guess both of us are avoiding it more or less. It's got to be talked about soon. Maybe I'm afraid it wouldn't be good for her to talk about it."

"Maybe it isn't good for her to keep all those feelings on the inside – you, too, for that matter," I suggested.

"Well, you've got a point there," he said, as he struggled to keep back the tears.

"Perhaps if we all talked together it would be easier," I offered.

At that point Jim nodded, and we walked toward the elevator.

In the room I opened the conversation almost immediately by asking about the surgery and what the physician told them.

Letha jumped at my invitation to talk about it in front of Jim. It was just like a wall of water rushing through a valley after the dam broke. She talked about her frightened feelings and her great sorrow for her husband.

This opened the way for Jim to reminisce about their life together. He shared how unbearable it was to think about Letha's possible death.

Finally the great waves of pain were calming and the two of them were ready to talk about the treatments.

Jim walked me to the front door of the hospital after the visit ended. He took my hand in both of his and said, "Larry, I thank you so much for coming all this way. I can never pay you, but I can tell you that you helped to start a beautiful dialogue between Letha and me. I'm sure that will be reward enough. There is a closeness now that should have been there before. Thank you. Thank you ever so much."

Jim was right. Self-disclosure in the family unit should not wait until a crisis is crashing down upon the family members.

2. Come to accept your own value as a person.

This concept is closely related to the first one. Until you feel good about yourself, you will not be comfortable about people knowing who you are. A major loss often causes a lowering of self-esteem. The restoration of self-esteem is much easier when the self-image is strong prior to the loss.

3. Take time to develop the inner person.

A classic example of this concept is the widow of six years who was my solace in times of stress. I was just a young intern-pastor in Ohio, causing many of my own crises due to inexperience and over-confidence. That didn't make a bit of difference to her. She always had a cold drink for me and plenty of time to listen to my woes.

She was more than a good listener, she was interested in so much of life. She was the most widely read person in the church. Any subject I brought up was a great importance to her. She had been developing the inner person for many years. Letters from all over the world were covering half of her dining room table. Needlework projects and handcrafted items adorned her walls.

When her husband died she went through the expected pain and sorrow, but adjustment came quite easily. You see, her interests were uniquely hers and not closely tied to her husband. She was a person in her own right. There was so much within her that could not die with the death of her husband.

4. Learn independence.

Floundering in unfamiliar responsibility that leads to anxiety is a good description of many grieving people who have been overly dependent upon the deceased.

Much of this could be prevented by deliberately learning independence before a major loss occurs.

A surprising number of older men leave the family finances and the food preparation entirely up to the wife. When they are widowed, they become unraveled.

Alex is a good example. I saw him on the front porch of his cottage every day. One day I saw a sign on the porch post that read "Free Kittens." My curiosity won out and I stopped to get acquainted.

Alex's wife died several years before. He was totally dependent on her for everything. His only act of independence was going to work every morning, but now that was mere memory.

Now his daughter was his sole source of support. She cleaned the house, brought in hot meals and took care of all of Alex's financial affairs.

One day the old man made the first independent decision he had made in years – he would start going to church. One problem. His daughter held the purse strings and feared that the old man would get "slap-happy" when the offering plate was passed.

"You go to church and you can make your own meals and clean your own house," she threatened.

Alex never went to church. To my knowledge he never resolved the grief over his wife's death.

With a little more independence he might have picked life up again and brought fulfillment to his later years.

5. Take time to do things together.

A friend of mine promised his wife that they'd go to Florida. His promise was repeated seven years in a row because he was too busy. His wife became ill and died after more than a year of hospitalizations. I can assure you that guilt plagued him for a long time.

Playing together, laughing and leisure time means fewer regrets and easier adjustment after death.

I have observed many people in grief. It seems to me that those who put a lot of living into their days and brought a lot of meaning into the lives of others by way of love, tenderness and expressions of appreciation, are the ones who make easier re-entry into life after the loss has been experienced.

6. Develop a realistic set of life-expectations.

Life is not a happy-forever-after situation. We are not immune to sickness, accident, separation and death. Both husband and wife do not necessarily live to be 85 in good health. There may be physical and emotional deficits along the way.

I remember how shocked I was when I began seeing little round spots crossing the windshield as I drove along the highway. I went to an eye doctor who told me I had floaters. He said it was typical of people who are aging. I was horrified. I had always had excellent vision. Floaters never crossed my mind, but when I told my friends about it they laughed. They also had floaters. Why should I be an exception?

A woman was upset when her husband had a stroke. Her husband would never drive again. They planned to travel ten months of the year and spend the other two in a cottage in Colorado. Now she had visions of visiting a nursing home for years to see her husband. She found out that life issues no unconditional guarantees.

Forever bliss is not realistic. Realizing this makes taking some of life's potholes much easier.

7. Put your heart into every day.

Live enthusiastically. Look at the people you live with and appreciate them. As Orville Kelley said, "Make today count." Don't spend much time Monday-morning-quarterbacking the past. Make a solid decision that you'll never judge your past performance by what you think you know today.

8. Learn what to expect.

After conducting classes and workshops on grief for almost two decades, I have had many people tell me that learning what to expect in times of loss definitely helped them cope with their respective losses.

Are you ready for a loss? Not entirely, but being informed about grief can reduce some of the surprise and fear.

Reflection Time

Complete after *Passages...through grief* session

Date: _____

What event or experience had an impact on you at the session tonight?

What feelings, thoughts, or insights did you notice?

What was helpful?

What were your feeling(s) in the closing circle?

Reflection Time

Date: _____

Think about your day today. What is a feeling you have felt (use **Feelings Chart** if help is needed for recognition)?

What event or experience had an impact on you?

What have you done for yourself?

Your thoughts or reactions:

Session Two

Session Two Information for Leaders

Welcoming New Participants

Ask new members to arrive before Session Two to register, be given materials, and a brief overview of Session One.

    If a new member arrives unannounced at the opening time of Session Two, ask them to stay afterwards to cover information.

    Make sure all members read and sign the "Group Contract."

    Assign new participants to a sharing group.

Passages Foundations (45-50 minutes)

Welcome

Moment of silence to recognize their courage

If new members are present, ask for a personal introduction of all participants and leaders, stressing brevity

- Name
- Loss that brings them to the program

Discuss **Responses to Grief** (homework assignment)

- Invite participants to share what responses were surprising or normalizing

Review **Grief is...** chart and clarify each point

- Refer to **Grief is...** chart p. 88

Read aloud **Grief is...**article p. 90 (PM p. 34)

- Clarify understanding.

Read aloud and discuss **Definitions for *Passages...through grief*** p. 92 (PM p. 36)

- These terms are used throughout the program, so a full understanding is important

Read aloud and discuss **The Grief Process** p. 93 (PM p. 37)
Discuss **Waves of Grief** poster p. 33

- How the waves can affect the griever
- Have them draw their own grief wave

Introduce **Depression Symptoms Scale** p. 94 (PM p. 38)

- Have them complete it at this time
- Invite them to talk with a leader after the session, if they are concerned about their responses
- Refer to **Red Flags** p. 7

Read aloud and discuss **Facing the Big Challenge** p. 95 (PM p. 39)

- Emphasize that personal commitment makes the difference
- Refer to **Taking Control** p. 12

Introduce **Identifying Your Strengths and Weaknesses** p. 97 (PM p. 41)
Have participants begin writing for 5 minutes, to get them moving on the assignment

Break (5 – 10 minutes)

At the end of break, each facilitator gathers their sharing group members and moves to their meeting space

- Members are to take their manuals
- Facilitators take the **Affirmation** poster

Sharing Group(s) (45 minutes)

Read aloud together the **Affirmation** poster
Ask about and support **small steps**
If the group needs guidance, offer discussion of:

- **Depression Symptoms Scale** results—were they surprised by their responses?
- Waves of grief—invite participants to relate their waves
- How was it to get through last week's session?

- What was it like to hear of the losses of other participants?
- What was it like for them to do the homework?

In Closing (15 minutes)

Identify the **Grief Clichés** activity to be completed for follow-up p. 98 (PM p. 42)
Review **Follow-up for the Week** (content)
Closing Ritual—gather participants into a circle and invite them to, "Name a feeling you've felt tonight." To create a quiet and accepting atmosphere, leaders and facilitators invite participants to join hands and close eyes.

- One leader begins by stating a feeling
- Allow for silence
- Do not expect everyone to participate
- Conclude after appropriate length of silence for sharing by saying, "Go in peace."

Post Session Meeting for Leaders and Facilitators

Review and discuss:

- Progress or difficulties of individual participants
    o Note referrals or other services needed
- The overall functioning of the whole group
- The overall functioning of the sharing group(s)
- Boundaries and responses to behaviors that detract from a healthy group (e.g., the excessive talking individual)
- Challenging responses to situations (e.g., comparing losses, person who doesn't share, very tearful person) that need addressing with the participant prior to the next session
    o Who will address participant
- Prepare weekly letters for each participant
    o Arrange for mailing

Provide support for each other!

Session Two Guide for Participants

Follow-up for the Week:

Complete *Grief Clichés*

Complete *Identifying Strengths and Weaknesses*

What are your *Challenges*?

Review *Small Steps*

Read Yeagley's articles:

"The Anatomy of Grief"

"Tasks of Grieving"

Use *Reflection Time* notes to support your writing for the week

Grief is... (Chart)

The **Grief is...** (Chart) is useful in teaching the basics of grief. Use the information following each term as descriptive and defining in the discussion.

- **Natural.** Grief is of nature, a part of the world. It is a response brought into being by the human mind. Not only is grief natural, but healing is as well. We are meant to heal, meant to recover.
- **Normal.** Grief comes from the feelings associated with the loss of something significant. We all have significant relationships in our lives, so we all have grief when loss occurs. The feelings of grief may feel very abnormal but aren't. They are a natural, normal response to loss.
- **Process.** Often society speaks of grief as an event, not a process. Others put a timeline on grief and have limited tolerance for grief reactions. In reality, the grief process should not be limited. It is the progression of taking feelings, emotions, and thoughts from one form to another. Processing grief is ongoing, active, and meant to evolve for the griever.
- **Difficult**. When we mention difficult, we look at the group and say, "You understand this." Grief affects a person spiritually, emotionally, physically, intellectually, and mentally. Grieving is just plain difficult.
- **Active.** Grieving requires action, energy, and involvement by the griever.
- **Self-centered.** Grief is in response to a loss affecting the self, so self-centeredness is natural, normal and necessary. Being self-centered is not selfish or negative. It provides a core from which to work. This core is a constant which allows feelings to move back and forth for healing.
- **Unique to you.** Each relationship with another is different, therefore each loss response and grief experience is different. The statement frequently used, "I know how you feel," is so wrong. **No-one** knows how another feels.
- **Result of a loss that mattered.** Grief is felt by those who have lost something or someone for whom they cared, loved, or had mixed feelings about. It is up to the griever, not others, to recognize the importance of the loss to them.
- **Has a beginning, a middle and an end.** The beginning is when the feelings of loss are first felt, the middle is the time of processing, and the end is when the pain of the loss is not the foremost response. The timeline is unique to the griever and is based on doing the necessary work of grieving. Hearing that the pain will end provides encouragement and motivation.

Grief is...

Natural

Normal

Process

Difficult

Active

Self-centered

Unique to you

Result of a loss

that mattered

Has a beginning, a middle and an end.

Grief is...

Something has happened that has thrown your life into crisis, turned everything upside down. Maybe someone has died, or your partner has left the relationship, or you have moved to a strange place, having to leave people who are important to you. That response you're having with a varied mix of feelings from anguish and deep sadness to anger and raw tenderness –that response is grief.

Like the intense pain that accompanies a physical wound, grief feelings are a signal that our emotional self has been deeply injured and needs tending before we can heal. It is both a normal and a natural reaction, even though it does not feel "right" at all.

When we grieve, we need understanding and support from others. First, we need to have others listen to us and validate our feelings. But it's risky to open up to others, because so often people in our society don't understand grief at all and so they are likely to expect us to be finished with our grief feelings long before we can be. We need to be heard but they give us clichés. We know that looking "strong" is really a façade. But others will accept the façade and not acknowledge the powerful impact of our loss. That is because Americans are encouraged to hide vulnerable feelings and pretend we're doing better than we really are. It can leave the griever alone, both physically and emotionally.

Healing any kind of deep wound results in a scar. That is true for healing emotional wounds, too. Scar tissue is quite strong even though it looks different from uninjured skin. Seeing a scar is a reminder of the original hurt. Like physical wounds, if the loss is tended, it heals appropriately and more thoroughly. The scar is less pronounced and the person is able to move into living a life with promise and meaning.

Grieving is healthy and natural. However, if we begin grieving and get others' clichés or non-supportive comments indicating their expectation that we should be "moving on," we wonder if we're doing it wrong. Or, if the reality of the loss is too powerful, we may feel overwhelmed and shut down emotionally. We may be reluctant to allow tears to flow and difficult emotions to be felt, so we get blocked. This blocking of grief is quite unhealthy. Unresolved grief experiences over the years cost us dearly in our ability to experience life fully. These costs may include difficulty with trust, inability to seek new healthy relationships, or trouble reaching acceptance and peace with our life situation.

Fear can accompany any life change...fear of the unknown, fear of loss, fear of not being able to stand up to a needed change and face it. Indeed, fear is a most common, difficult feeling that affects the ways we think and behave. When fear is directing us, whether we are aware of it or not, we are not behaving in our own, true best interest. Fear can grip us so that we lose perspective. The fight and flight reactions to fearful situations are well-known, natural reactions for immediate crises. But like a physical crisis, when the instant has passed, tending to the aftermath is key. So during a time of grief, fear that takes the form of anger or acting-out behaviors will block recognition of how grief really feels. Similarly, many a griever may get overly involved in work activities or travels or other escapes that prevent their grief from being observed. When we block grief, we avoid healing.

Healthy grieving requires us to face the pain and fears and work through them. There are supports, like this ***Passages...through grief*** program with readings and group sharing that encourage us to deal with our losses. Grieving in a healthy way is a decision, and it requires courage to follow through. The major steps we need to take in order to heal are...

- understanding the primary elements of a healthy grief
- talking and writing about our feelings
- being heard as we process our unfinished business

Definitions for *Passages...through grief*

Grief: The incompatible feelings resulting from a loss that mattered.

Process: The combination of experiences and feelings over time that is included in the grief journey.

Processing: The work of intentionally thinking, talking and feeling the different aspects of grief.

Recovery: Recognizing and completing the unfinished business of the loss.

> **Grief lasts from**
>
> **when loss is first felt**
>
> **until the pain**
>
> **is not the primary focus.**

The Grief Process

Knowing what to expect in grief helps us feel more normal and can be reassuring. Experiencing major changes, including loss, initially strikes us acutely and brings numbing shock. This is often followed by very powerful feelings that are overwhelming. It is like wading in calm ocean water, gradually sensing a strange pull from beneath you and then being slammed with a huge wave that thrashes and pulls you under and around in a chaos of confusion and helplessness only to be left alone once again on the still shore.

We describe this experience as **wavelike**, where one is inundated by very intense, overwhelming anguish that lasts a minute or an hour. Tears and pain then subside, leaving one in a tender calm space where there is fatigue but release. Like the ocean, these waves of grief may be very strong one time and much milder another. The whole process is the struggle of our emotional self-adapting to something that is very difficult to accept. A battle is going on inside, pushing and pulling as we fight the reality of loss. We want it not to be true, and we wrestle valiantly to change it back even as we gradually comprehend the truth. When the calmer times come, we may believe the battle is over and we are doing fine, and then another wave will strike in a different way. So the wavelike grief process is uneven and erratic.

And this is all very normal and healthy.
In the space below create your wave of grief.

People often experience depressed feelings during grief. Complete this scale to note areas needing your attention. If you have troubling concerns, please tell someone and get help for yourself

Depression Symptoms Scale

Date: _____

Place a check under the number that indicates where you think you fit at this time.

0 = no problem   **10 = big problem**

Symptom	0	1	2	3	4	5	6	7	8	9	10
Tired most of the time											
General feeling of weakness											
Worried about the next thing you must do.											
Crying/tearfulness											
Poor memory											
Loss of self-esteem											
Changes in sleep pattern											
Agitated, restless, tense											
Overwhelming sadness											
Feeling unworthy or guilty											
Unable to concentrate											
Feelings of abandonment											
Changes in eating pattern											
Lost interest in former pleasant activities											

Facing the Big Challenge

The grief experience can feel huge. Defining different ways to approach it, can make this Big Challenge possible. We begin with the question:

How will I fit what has happened into the rest of my life?

Address challenging questions.

- What adjustments are necessary for daily living?
- What will I do now?
- What do I need help with?
- Who will help me?
- What do I need to do to get to the next step?
- What would I like to have done/accomplished during this hard time?
- What do I need to overcome?
- What is *incomplete* about the relationship or situation that I need to finish?

Address your fears.

- What fears stand in my way?
- My fears are real but are they true?

Recognize your own courage.

Some people call it nerve, some call it guts. Courage is taking <u>one</u> <u>small</u> <u>step</u> toward meeting the challenge, like:

- Pushing yourself to do things you fear or feel you are unable to do
- Trying something new
- Letting tears flow until they cease on their own
- Asking someone to listen to your story for the first time

Courage does not mean taking giant leaps into an unknown deep end of the pool. Courage means taking small steps every day, usually uncomfortable at first, that go in the direction you want to go, toward where you want to be (in time).

Find ways to encourage recovery.

- Look for others who have grown through grief and made a meaningful life. Let them model and give hope for the grief journey.
- Attend a grief program like *Passages...through grief* or a group which will provide understanding and a sense of support.
- Learn and apply skills of self-care - meditation, walking, journaling, massage, or cuddling a favorite pet - anything that is comforting and encouraging.
- Read stories of the grief journeys of others.
- Recall difficult times overcome in the past. What personal strengths were helpful through those times?

Identifying Strengths and Weaknesses

Personal strengths and weaknesses have an impact on surviving and managing grief. In the past, you have had difficult times or events. Using the chart below, name an event and remember how you dealt with it. Identify the strengths you used (e.g., asking others to listen, learning about grief).

In addition to strengths, we each have weaknesses. Again, take the difficult time or event in your past and identify what you wish you could have done (e.g., your inability to ask for help or unwillingness to share with others).

When you complete the chart, read through what you have written. What are the strengths you recognize? Have you changed a weakness into a strength (e.g., from isolating yourself to sharing with others)?

My Strengths and Weaknesses

Difficult Time or Event	Weakness	Strength

Grief Clichés

People often use clichés when talking with those who have had a significant loss. What do you think about these clichés? There is space following each for your reactions.

"Time heals all wounds."

"Keep busy."

"It was God's will." or *"God needed another angel in heaven."*

"He or She lived a good long life."

"You need to be strong for others."

"I know just how you feel."

"We're never given more than we can handle."

"You must be strong for your children."

Implied comment – "Just replace what was lost."

"Call me if there is anything I can do."

What comments have people said to you that were hurtful?

What do you wish people <u>would</u> say to you?

Yeagley's

"The Anatomy of Grief"

I decided to visit the residents in the complex for senior citizens located across from my church. I'm glad I did, particularly because I met Mr. Haskins. He had been working in the kitchen when I rang his doorbell. He showed me to a seat and returned to the kitchen.

"I don't mean to be rude," he called from the kitchen, "but I've got to watch my eggs or else they'll burn. I'm not the best hand at this. Never had to do it before to this extent."

There was a clattering of pans and more talking that I couldn't make out. Finally Mr. Haskins entered the living room carrying a tray with his piping hot lunch. He placed the tray on a small table, pulled a rocking chair up to it and sat down. He bowed his head reverently and soon proceeded to eat.

"You may think it eccentric of me to eat my meal in the living room like this. Maybe you'd understand if I told you that my wife died a short while ago. I sat in the kitchen with her and ate my meals with her for the last 40 years. Now that she's gone I can't bear to eat in the kitchen. It brings back too many memories. I just won't be the same again," he told me between sobs.

As I listened to Mr. Haskins, I realized that his whole life had become out of focus. He had lost his equilibrium. Without his wife, there seemed to be no purpose in living another day. He ate, but nothing tasted good. He tried to sleep, but sleep seldom came. During the day he was able to drop off to sleep in his old rocker, but he was awakened by dreams of his wife. He had nobody to talk with. Once in a while the visiting nurse came by, but it was a different one most of the time. The person he related to the best was now gone. Life was so empty.

Thousands of people just like Mr. Haskins are in grief. Some have a pretty good idea of what to expect, but most of them enter grief without prior knowledge of what it is like. They are frightened and sometimes worry about losing their sanity.

If you are having these fears in your time of grief, let me assure you that grief is a normal and healthy reaction to a great loss. It is the attempt of the person to bring about equilibrium...the attempt to be whole again.

There is no stereotype in grief, no one way for it to happen. Each person is unique in his makeup and each person grieves in a unique way. God ministers to each person in a unique way.

A woman looked at another woman in a therapy group and said, "I don't think I'll ever get over this. Look at me. I'm falling apart. It's been eight months since John died and I'm just as bad off now as I was the week of his death. But here is Mildred. She lost her husband about the same time I lost mine. Is she suffering? Why, she is miles ahead of me."

The therapist quickly asked the woman if she might not be making an unfair comparison. Further conversation among member of the group revealed that the cases of the two women were entirely different.

In the next few minutes the people in the therapy group built a list of factors that had a bearing on the nature of grief. I'll share that list with you.

The age of the grieving person. Younger people have larger circles of supporting relationships to help in times of loss. Advancing age narrows those circles and limits the opportunities of building new relationships. Age also may have an influence on the general health of the individual. Poor health may hinder recovery from a major loss.

My father wasn't able to adjust to my mother's death. He would look at her picture on the wall and order her to make his meal. His age and physical condition prevented him from reinvesting in life.

The manner of the death. Many people in the group agreed with the woman who lost a son through suicide that this would be the most difficult grief. Sudden and tragic death was considered extremely difficult to cope with. Death of an infant or a young child came very close to the death of a young parent in terms of painful adjustment. Long term illness that leaves a person emaciated or deformed was felt to be extremely difficult for the survivors, particularly if they had a part in the ill person's care resulting in their fatigue prior to the death.

During my hospital chaplain days I saw children in the emergency room who had been run over by a parent. This type of death is so devastating that the lives of parents and grandparents are in jeopardy. I have seen entire families come to a screeching halt.

Previous warning. Some people in the group told about doing much of their grieving before the death, which seemed to lessen the suffering of grief after death. Previous warning didn't seem to help matters if the family and the dying person couldn't bring themselves to talk openly about the imminent death. The lack of openness and intimacy in these cases produced guilt that inhibited the grieving. On the other hand, people who put extra amounts of quality into those last days or weeks were reporting an easier time in their grief.

I worked in hospices for years. I've noticed that families who have lost a loved one less than six months after diagnosis seemed to have a more difficult time in grief. Those who lost approximately two years after diagnosis also seemed to adjust slowly. In the former case there seems to be much denial. In the latter case there are unrealistic expectations arising from numerous rallies after many crises. The best adjustments appeared to take place when loss occurred six to eighteen months after diagnosis.

The personality of the survivor. Some people are very dependent in a relationship. When death occurs they find adjustment too full of responsibilities for which they are not prepared. The independent person may have an easier time adjusting.

Life experiences while growing up. There seemed to be some evidence that people who experienced a number of deprivations in the formative years were better equipped to handle losses of all sorts.

Relationships and interaction with the person who died. A general feeling in the group was that grief went well if the relationship with the person who died went well. People in longstanding grief situations are frequently heard to lament, "If only I could have another chance...just a few more months to show her that I really did love her" or "It wouldn't be so bad if I hadn't hated him so much of the time."

While the nature of grief is different for each person, there are also some fairly common denominators in all grief. I hesitate to call them steps or stages. Perhaps the situation is one of moving from one reaction to another, sometimes with no rhyme or reason.

Here are some of the reactions I have observed in groups I have facilitated:

Confusion

I frequently draw a large circle on the blackboard to represent a grieving person. Inside the circle I draw many arrows pointing in many directions. The arrows represent the many conflicting, painful, upsetting and contradictory emotions. At the top of the circle I write the CONFUSION.

Shock and Numbness

Shock and numbness are very early experiences in grief. Some authors say that shock lasts from two hours to two days, but I have seen people in a dazed condition weeks after the death of a loved one. Trying to recall the activities of the first few weeks after the death may be next to impossible for them.

I remember a thin woman in her eighties sitting in the emergency room family area. The doctor announced very kindly that her husband died. She sat there as if nothing had been said. The doctor told her he was going to return to seeing other patients, but that he would gladly return if she had any questions. For a few moments she flew at the doctor with both fists swinging. Quickly she apologized and returned to her chair. She sat there in silence and shock for over an hour. Her family arrived and led her to a car. She looked like she had been drugged.

Shock may well be a God-given anesthetic that prevents sudden death upon hearing the news of another person's death.

I've seen the shock in cases of divorce announcements, job losses and broken romances.

Disbelief

A common defense mechanism is stubborn disbelief. Some professionals call it denial. It begins very early in the experience of loss.

A friend of mine went to the hospital to see her father. She didn't know that her father had died. The hospital was unable to reach her because she was in transit to the hospital. She looked through the window of the intensive care unit and saw the family gathered around the bed. The minister was there. Her first impulse was to run out of that hospital so that nobody could tell her. If she wasn't told she wouldn't have to believe it. For her, denial and shock were instantaneous reactions to death.

Fear

Paralyzing fear and dread are reported by many people. Some fear the next event in life. Others fear being alone. The fear of darkness is reported.

Anger

Anger is also prevalent in grief. People are angry at the doctor, the nurse, the hospital, the minister, the person who died, and even at themselves. Anger against God is frequently noticed.

I was traveling in a foreign country a few years ago when I met a teacher who asked me to see his friend when I returned to the United States. His friend, a young mother of three children, had a series of deaths in her immediate family. The latest death was that of her young son. She was terribly angry at God, but the people in her church shamed her for having such feelings. What a relief it was for her to discover that God was just as interested in hearing about her anger as He was her joy. She talked about her anger to me and she talked to God about it. The result...reconciliation with God.

Depression

When denial, anger and extracting promises from God do not change the situation of loss, many people become depressed. This is characterized by feelings of hopelessness, helplessness, despair, resignation, lethargy and intense searching for the missing. Loss of appetite, sleeplessness and disinterest in everything except thoughts of the dead are often noticed. Headaches, backaches, tightening feelings around the chest, feeling that food tastes like sand, inadequate saliva to moisten food, and feelings of nausea are frequently reported. Feelings of exhaustion make it nearly impossible to lift one foot up after the other. Concentration on anything other than the lost love object is unthinkable. Usual abilities to organize things seem to vanish. The term "out of focus" is the best way to summarize it.

Over a period of ten years I asked people in groups to rate themselves on depression symptoms. The results were surprisingly similar from one group to another. Every single group placed sadness at the top of the list. Inability to concentrate and remember was always high on the list, along with dislike for pleasures that were appealing prior to the loss.

The emotions and psychosomatic symptoms just described in detail are part of the normal range of reactions to loss. Given time and adequate support, the period of acute pain will pass and restored equilibrium will be a believable reality.

Adjustment cannot be charted as a steadily ascending line. There are setbacks along the way. Holidays and anniversaries have a way of causing regression, but the renewed suffering is not nearly as intense as it was earlier.

C.S. Lewis, in his book *A Grief Observed*, said, "Grief is like a long valley, a winding valley where any bend may reveal a totally new landscape. Not every bend does. Sometimes the surprise is the opposite one; you are presented with exactly the same sort of country you thought you had left behind miles ago. That is when you wonder whether the valley isn't a circular trench. But it isn't. There are partial recurrences, but the sequence doesn't repeat."

Grief is not to be shunned or escaped. Sooner or later it is experienced. To those who have lost a loved one through death or divorce, or to those who face their own death, I would say, "Let grief happen. It is not an enemy to be silenced. It does not lead to despair, but to growthfulness."

Yeagley's
"Tasks of Grieving"

The developing science of thanatology has spawned scores of 'how-to' books on grief. Some of them have produced some misconceptions about the components of grief. I read about "phases of grief," "stages of grief," and "steps of grief." Shock, denial, anger, fear, bargaining, depression, and acceptance are commonly mentioned reactions. This systematization of grief is problematic when it gives the misconception that everyone must go through the "phases" one at a time before grieving has really happened.

It is much less problematic to think about the four tasks that are usually accomplished as people move from recent loss to adjustment.

First Task

The first task is coming to the place where you consider the loss a reality. There is no progress toward regaining your equilibrium until this is done.

One day a young woman who heard about my work walked into my office. Her whole life was a long series of losses. Her latest loss was the death of her teenager. She'd say things like, "If Eddie ever died I don't know how I could handle it." I could talk to her about any other loss, but she refused to talk about Eddie. If I pressed her ever so gently, she would say, "I refuse to talk about that. Eddie isn't dead and I won't talk that way."

Sometimes people preserve bedrooms or workshops just as they were the day of the death. They tell themselves that their loved ones are on a trip for a few days. They cannot perform the next tasks of grieving until they have said, "I know he is dead and won't be coming back."

At the close of a therapy session a woman said, "You know, I think I am finally beginning to heal."

"How can you tell?" I asked.

"My husband died two months ago in the Brighton hospital. Every day since then I have called the head nurse on the cancer floor and asked how Barney is doing. Every day the nurse quietly reminded me that Barney had died. But I didn't call the hospital once this week. I know Barney died. I believe it now. That's why I can tell that I am beginning to heal."

Second Task

The second task of grief is to be willing to experience the pain and suffering caused by a major disruption in life.

Nobody gets excited about pain. It is almost instinctive to withdraw from anything that is accompanied by discomfort. People in grief are no exception.

As I work with groups of grief stricken people, I can be ever so gentle, yet some will hesitate to attend the second session because of the pain. A few even say that the group meeting caused them to have a regression.

I am discovering that people who make these objections usually have avoided all thoughts, situations and sights that would cause the slightest pain. When they attend a group meeting where people are sharing the nature of their losses and where painful feelings are expressed, it sends their own painful feelings cascading into the consciousness of the mind. Then they feel a strong urge to run from the pain.

Pain must be experienced if healing is to occur. Pain must be expressed if growth and new life are to result.

I have frequently observed small children receiving an injury, physical or emotional, when the parents were not around. They show the hurt for a few minutes, but fight back the tears. Then a parent arrives on the scene. The child runs to the parent and breaks down in tears. They finally express the pain experienced earlier. What relief. What healing.

In grief, pain is a sign of healing. Feeling and expressing pain is healthy and absolutely essential.

My friends who work with people who have suffered major losses agree that when people can't or won't experience and express pain, they become stalemated. Progress toward recovery is halted.

Going through pain has a way of mellowing the pain. The sharp sting is lessened. Eventually thoughts of the loss evoke mostly good and warm memories. Now the person is ready for the third task of grief.

Third Task

The third task of grief is to move back into the familiar environment associated with the person who is now gone.

A friend of mine worked in the same establishment where her husband worked. After he had divorced her, she was devastated with pain every day she went to work. It was not until she had freely expressed and worked through her pain that she could walk into her place of employment with her head held high.

Some people travel, work a second job, or stay with friends and relatives to avoid going home after the loss of a spouse or child. Young people may leave home or run the streets to avoid going home to a house where a loved one is missing.

All of us move back into familiar environments differently. Some do it gradually and some do it abruptly. The important thing is to do the tasks without getting bogged down.

A friend of mine was comfortable in the home where she and her husband had lived together, but she couldn't look out the window at the fruit trees her husband had planted before his death. She often screamed as she walked from the car to the house. The orchard was an acutely painful part of her surroundings long after she had adjusted to other aspects of her loss.

She finally took a memory trip through the history of the orchard as it related to her husband. She wrote about the orchard in her journal and talked about it to friends. Eventually she was able to walk among the trees, touch the boughs with her hands, and talk aloud about the part her husband played in the planting of the trees. Within weeks she was able to enjoy walking in the orchard.

If you discover a part of your world that causes pain, don't permit this to discourage you. The pace of adjustment is not all that important. The key to recovery is actively grieving as soon as possible... small step by small step.

Fourth Task

The fourth task is saying good-bye. This is the slow process of withdrawing the mountains of emotional energy invested in the lost relationship and reinvesting that energy in other relationships.

Some people call this psychological amputation. Perhaps this is their way of saying that "letting go" or "saying good-bye" to a loved one is a major shock to the system. On the other hand, amputation is sometimes the only way to save a person's life. This is true in grief. The only way you can be free to go on living in a satisfying manner is to say good-bye to the relationship that can no longer be.

Scores of people who attend support groups report that they had to say good-bye before they really began to live again. This is not to say that they discarded their memories. Memories are symbols of love. Saying good-bye is admitting and acting on the fact that a present relationship with a lost person cannot be productive. It is accepting the fact that living in the past is cheating you and others who could benefit from your fellowship.

You do not withdraw all the emotional energy in a lost relationship. Instead you keep a small investment in memories of the person you lost. Now you relate to that person as missing, not alive as before. You can reminisce and talk about him or her with pleasure. And this new type of emotional attachment does not keep you from forming other friendships. Once again you can engage in a variety of life pursuits.

Reflection Time

Complete after *Passages...through grief* session

Date: _____

What event or experience had an impact on you at the session tonight?

What feelings, thoughts, or insights did you notice?

What was helpful?

What were your feeling(s) in the closing circle?

Reflection Time

Date: _____

Think about your day today. What is a feeling you have felt (use **Feelings Chart** if help is needed for recognition)?

What event or experience had an impact on you?

What have you done for yourself?

Your thoughts or reactions:

Session Three

Session Three Information for Leaders

Passages Foundations (45-50 minutes)

Welcome
Moment of silence to recognize their courage
Review **Grief Clichés**—homework assignment

- Encourage participants to share
- Refer to **Reality of Grief Clichés** p. 115

Read aloud **Grief is...** p. 119 (PM p. 61)

- Encourage questions

Review **Short Term Relievers of Grief** p. 120 (PM p. 62)

- Refer to **Self-care** p. 116
- Clarify understanding of "short-term"

Review **Self-care Relievers of Grief** p. 121 (PM p. 63)

- Highlight examples of living in the "present moment"

Review and discuss **The Holidays and Special Days** p. 123 (PM p. 65)

- Ask participants to share their days of challenge
- Invite them to claim a self-care strategy

Recognize **The Grief of Children and Teens** p. 125 (PM p. 67)

- If this is pertinent to the participants, discuss openly

Complete **Stress Test** p. 127 (PM p. 69)

- Ask for reactions
- Reiterate need for self-care
- Refer to **Red Flags** p. 7

Break (5 – 10 minutes)

At end of break, each facilitator gathers their sharing group members and moves to their meeting space

- Members are to take their manuals
- Facilitators take the **Affirmation** poster

Sharing Group(s) (45 minutes)

Read aloud together the **Affirmation** poster
Ask about and support "small steps"
If the group needs guidance, offer discussion of:

- **Stress Test** results
- Did their homework bring up reactions or insights?
- Self-care:
    o How do you need to take care of yourself?
    o Ask what they currently do for self-care and what they would like to try

In Closing (15 minutes)

Give directions for **My Loss History** pp. 129-130 (PM pp. 71-72)

- Refer to **Assignments that Require a Listener** p. 4
- The assignment will need to be completed for use next week

Note **Follow-up for the Week** (content)
Lead **Guided Visualization** p. 117
Gather participants in a closing circle

> A Leader demonstrates the rubber band metaphor: using a thick rubber band, stretch it out fully and compare it to our being in a stress mode. Note that we can be stretched to the maximum, briefly. Extend and release the rubber band to show how we are meant to be able to handle stress and return to a calmer base to recoup. Note further if held in a strained stretch of stress, we, like the rubber band, will break.

Closing Ritual - invite participants to "Name a feeling you've felt tonight." To create a quiet and accepting atmosphere, join hands and close eyes.

- One leader begins by stating a feeling
- Allow for silence
- Do not expect everyone to participate
- Conclude after appropriate length of silence for sharing by saying, "Go in peace."

Post Session Meeting for Leaders and Facilitators

Review and discuss:

- How this group is coming together
- The progress of individuals
- Difficulties of individual participants
    o Who will discuss issues with the participant before the next session
    o Referrals or other services needed
- Prepare weekly letters for each participant
    o Arrange for mailing

Provide support for each other!

Grief Clichés

In our opinion these "Grief Clichés" are hurtful and should be *forbidden*. They are given in an open format for participant discussion. We have added comments that may be useful in guiding this discussion.

"Time heals all wounds." Time alone does not heal. Allowing yourself to work through the pain and feelings about the loss, and completing the relationship you had with the lost person or situation, leads to healing over time.

"Keep busy." Keeping busy keeps feelings away. This avoidance uses energy and makes you tired.

"It was God's will." or *"God needed another angel in heaven."* When hearing this, some people find it difficult to believe in a God who loves them or have difficulty continuing the relationship they have had with God.

"He or She lived a good long life." The loss of someone important to you matters whatever the age.

"You need to be strong for others." Grievers do the best they can. Trying to be strong all the time leads to unresolved grief and physical ailments from the stress on the body, mind, and spirit.

"I know just how you feel." **No one** has the feelings you have. Others may have had similar losses but they **cannot** know how you feel.

"We're never given more than we can handle." There are times when situations in life can be more than one is able to handle **alone**.

"Just replace the _____ (what was lost)." The feelings and the relationship of the loss need to be grieved before one can go forward with new healthy relationships.

"You must be strong for your children." Children need to witness grief from the key adults in their lives. If they see grief in healthy ways through crying, feeling sad, seeking others to provide support, it gives them permission to grieve as well. When feelings are given words, it helps youngsters identify their own feelings. It is important for the adult to have adult support, so children are not called on to be that support.

"Call me if there is anything I can do." These words are so generic and are usually said by those who care, but don't know what to do. When overwhelmed by grief, it may be difficult to respond to this comment. A goal might be to call and ask the person offering help to do a specific task that would offer relief (ex., mowing the lawn, providing transportation, stacking wood, etc.).

In response to *"What do you wish people <u>would</u> say to you?"* some participants grieving a death loss have said they long for people to share a memory they have of the person who has died.

Self-Care

We find that the average participant of **Passages...through grief** does a poor job of providing healthy self-care. It could be that caregiving of others takes precedence; time is an issue; they feel it is selfish to "treat" themselves to care; or they don't feel they are worth the effort. Whatever the reason, self-care is essential to the wellness of a person. As leaders, it is one of our major tasks to convey the importance and value of taking care of the self. We've stated that grief is the hardest work a person can do. So when work is hard, it is necessary to take breaks, utilize self-care, and rest to provide the body, mind, and soul with the ability to do the work.

There are two articles presented in Session Three which focus on caring for the self. The first, "Short-Term Relievers of Grief" p. 120 (PM p. 62) identifies ways that grievers seek to ease or block their pain. These ways are normal and may be somewhat useful and relieving. But, the key is that they must be used moderately and for a limited time only. Adopting regular use, using excessively, or for extended periods are red flags of complications. Instead of dealing with grief, the griever will then have to deal with the results of their excesses. This, of course, pushes away their grief healing. Leaders need to stress this information to participants, and encourage seeking professional help if they are using short-term relievers to an excess or feel unable to care for themselves.

The second article, "Self-care Relievers of Grief" p. 121 (PM p. 63) emphasizes the necessity for caring for the self in healthy ways. The introductory statement regarding self-care vs. selfishness needs strong emphasis by the leaders. People often need "permission" to take on tasks that feel good and provide relief to them. Hearing that it is necessary, will help encourage those who are not utilizing self-care presently. At the bottom of the box is a balancing fulcrum for the continuum of selfless to selfish behavior. This is used to underscore that when any movement is made from "selflessness" toward being more "self-centered," it **feels** wrong, even though it is healthier. This example strikes a chord with caregivers.

The closing statement, "Your goal is to live in the present moment with the activity you choose," calls for explanation. This concept is profound and represents a mindset of living in the present and focusing on this moment. Participants will need encouragement in making the effort to adopt this mindset. Examples and referring to the process at other times during the program will be helpful in reinforcing this growth step.

Leaders, make it a point to ask the participants each week if they have used means of self-care. Celebrate their accomplishments and provide them with continued encouragement.

Guided Visualization

To begin, ask participants to:
"Sit in a comfortable position with your feet on the floor."

Once participants are relaxed and breathing calmly, say:
Imagine yourself in a quiet and peaceful place in nature." (Allow time to pass.)
"Gradually notice the sights, sounds, and smells of your surroundings." (Allow 1-2-3 minutes of silence.)
"You may return to this peaceful place any time you wish. And now you can come back to this room, little by little, and open your eyes to the count of three." (Allow several moments for participants to complete their quiet time.)

Leaders may find that their group responds well to these moments of quiet-taking and visualizations. If so, this process may well be used during other sessions.

Session Three Guide for Participants

Follow-up for the Week:

Complete *My Loss History* chart
Review *Small Steps*
Read Yeagley's articles:
    "Intentional Grieving"
    "Be Good to Yourself"
Use *Reflection Time* notes to support your writing for the week

Grief is...

When grief is new, we are gripped by moments of pain and anguish, and cannot imagine that we are involved in a process that has any kind of recognizable pattern. Each of us experiences grief uniquely. The process can be described as erratic and wavelike. That is, at times you may feel overwhelmed by the pain's intensity. Then other times you feel stronger than the pain and imagine you're getting through grief, only to be later caught up in its anguish again or in a new way, wondering if you've made any progress at all. Grief's waves are erratic, as are the episodes of pain relative to grief. The waves vary in three ways:

Intensity

Frequency

Duration

We've already referred to <u>intensity</u> as the power or strength of pain, sadness, anguish, or hurt. The <u>frequency</u> refers to how often we face painful episodes. Once beyond the initial shock of a loss, pain tends to move into our focus frequently and remain for long periods, which refers to the <u>duration</u> of an episode. As we learn to expect these episodes, we can be assured that the mixed and strong reactions are normal. The initial waves of grief are harsh and intense. Over time, the intensity, frequency, and duration of these waves will generally decrease. As we look for support in the midst of grief, we recognize that **healing comes from going through the pain.**

The brain has the key role in processing our pain. Understanding how it works is useful in differentiating thoughts and feelings. The most highly developed part of our brain is called the cerebral cortex, where we accomplish our <u>thinking</u>, calculating and understanding of ideas. On the other hand, the <u>feeling</u> center is located lower in the back of the brain, called the limbic system. **Our feelings lag behind thinking, and so our thoughts make sense to us long before our feelings agree.** Therefore, we need to continue with appropriate behaviors and self-reassurances, so our feelings can catch up and adjust to our thinking.

Facing our grief and dealing with the pain of loss or the confusion of change, takes courage. Yes, <u>courage</u>. In our world people are not taught how to grieve or that it is key to healing. And we have not learned from past experiences that we have the strength to do the work. So, even though grieving is normal and natural, it is most often not supported by people around us (after the first month). In order to heal we must gather **the courage to grieve.**

Short-Term Relievers of Grief

A list of **Short-Term Relievers of Grief** are given below.

These can be a comfort if used for a short time and in a very limited way.

If used extensively, grief gets blocked

and the healing process can become complicated.

Unhealthy eating
Sleeping excessively or not enough
Using sleeping pills
Becoming isolated or withdrawn
Engaging in high risk behaviors (i.e. gambling, speeding, fighting)
Using alcohol or drugs (illegal or prescription)
Excessive exercising
Mismanaging feelings of anger or planning revenge
Escaping mentally (i.e. movies, TV, books, games)
Excessive shopping or overspending
Compulsive working
Keeping "over busy"
Talking excessively
Escaping through travel
Compulsive cleaning or organizing

Self-Care Relievers of Grief

Passages...through grief differentiates between
being <u>self-centered</u> and being <u>selfish</u>.
Being self-centered
refers to being grounded or balancing the self
in constructive, healthy ways.
It is **not selfish** to take care of yourself.
It is healthy and necessary.

<u>Selflessness</u>   <u>Self-centered</u>   <u>Selfishness</u>

Below is a list of healthy ways to care for yourself that
are nourishing and foster the healing process.

Getting enough sleep
Eating well and slowly
Taking vitamins, adding a stress complex tablet
Avoiding excessive amounts of caffeine
Recognizing that alcohol, cigarettes, tranquilizers, and other drugs increase stress
    not reduce it
Including regular exercise in your schedule
Including enjoyable activities in your schedule
Having fun without feeling guilty!
Writing down your feelings on a daily basis
Reaching out to people who are good listeners
Seeking others who have had losses for mutual support
Identifying people who will respond to your request for help
Meditating
Singing alone or with a group
Taking bubble baths - with or without candles, music, incense
Dancing - alone or with others
Gardening
Kayaking, canoeing, or boating
Getting and giving hugs

Praying
Hearing birdsongs
Writing poetry
Getting massages
Breathing deeply
Using guided visualization
Taking long walks
Listening to peaceful music
Playing with clay
Making a secret surprise for someone
Laughing
Buying yourself a bouquet of flowers
Cuddling a pet
Crying to howling
Painting
Swinging
Listening to the waves
Getting a manicure/pedicure
Avoiding important decisions while in the most difficult times of grief

***Your goal is to live in the present moment
with the activity you choose.***

The Holidays and Special Days

Confusion or Celebration – Which is it for you?

Holidays and special days provide an extra challenge to grievers. When a holiday season approaches, the whole world seems consumed with celebrations, family, and sharing. Those who are grieving life's hurts often face a period of increased pain and loneliness. One woman declared, "I just want to dig a hole, climb in, pull the covers over top of me, and go to sleep until all the hullabaloo is over!" Many grieving people can relate to this woman's outcry!

Not only are holidays usually stressful, but hurting people have physical and emotional limitations that prevent them from functioning at their fullest. The "Responses to Grief" in Session One makes clear the numerous challenges. Confusion, questioning "Why?" and feeling overwhelmed often accompany approaching special days and holidays.

There are some tender days in the life of a grieving person that may not even be recognized as special to others around them. These days may include the wedding anniversary of a now divorced person, the death date, the anniversary of an illness diagnosis, the pregnancy due date of a premature child who died – the list is non-ending. Only grievers are able to define which dates hold significance for them. These dates may be anticipated with dread and may bring painful memories. The import of these days needs to be shared or they may usher in an increased sense of pain and loneliness.

The approach of the event may be more challenging than the actual day itself. The dread of feeling the memories is very difficult. It takes courage, strength and support to be active in this process. This is an expected part of grief. Tell yourself that through feeling the memories, you are helping yourself heal.

The following suggestions for coping may help provide *a sense of control* of a holiday or special day:

- Mark the difficult days on your calendar.
- Plan in advance how you will recognize these days.
- Answer whether you want the day to pass without recognition from others, or you would benefit from companionship and support?
- If you would like companionship, make a plan with a friend who will recognize the importance of this event and will allow you to share memories and feelings without trying to "fix you."

- If you desire time alone, consider what you will do with your time:
  - Read
  - Watch a special movie
  - Have a massage or other special treat
  - Take a long walk
  - Meditate
  - Spend time enjoying nature's beauty
  - Listen to music
  - Dedicate time to helping others
  - Take a trip out of town
- For holidays such as Christmas, Thanksgiving or Easter, consider whether you will find comfort in using old traditions or starting new ones. Discuss your choice with family or friends well in advance.
- Recognize your physical and emotional limitations. Do not try to do too much.
- Recognize the importance of self-care during this time.
- Rely on others to do the holiday preparations if you feel they are needed. People will be happy to have something to do that can be helpful to you. It may be the opportunity they have been awaiting.
- Consider letting go of holiday preparations.

The Grief of Children and Teens*

Adults may not recognize children's grief responses, and may not know what to say or do at such a time. They may have a need to "fix it" rather than allow children to move through their grief. So the grief is not addressed and children are left alone with their feelings. They are easily overlooked. In fact, children present their grief in different ways than adults. For instance, a sad and helpless feeling child may act out angrily.

Children develop the ability to express feelings as they age and are taught. When a loss occurs, the child may not know how to speak of their emotions. This often leaves their adults unaware of the feelings and turmoil that are present. Use of a "feelings chart" like the one offered in Session One may be most useful.

In *Passages...through grief* we have identified that adults who are grieving experience a lack of support and understanding. This holds for children as well. In addressing how children grieve, think of the lessons learned thus far in *Passages...through grief*. These same lessons about the process and means of self-support directed to adults, also pertain to children.

Adults are instrumental in providing the affirmation and support that a child requires. With these, children are able to emote and learn how to deal with feelings in a healthy manner. Often the parent(s) of a child are grieving as well, and may not be able to be the sole support person(s) for the child. If that is the case, seek mentorship from another caring adult.

Below is material to consider when dealing with grieving children. Adaptation to the child's age, personality, cognitive ability and maturity level will be necessary.

- There are numerous resources online to guide in understanding the grief responses of children. If an adult questions the appropriateness of a response or behavior, seek counsel with a grief counselor or therapist trained in children's grief, or a pediatrician.
- Provide them with the truth about the loss, in age-appropriate, simple terms. If the truth is not provided, children fill in the blanks with information that may be more painful and scary.
- LISTEN. Do not judge or give solutions to what a child should think or feel. Just allow them to talk and feel as they need. Do not try to "fix" him or her. Directions or options may be offered at a later time when the child asks.
- Be ready to address all questions asked using brief, age-appropriate answers. Do not give too much information at once, as it can be overwhelming. Instead, let them lead in asking for information. If they sense your willingness to listen and provide

honest answers, the child will ask what he or she needs to know in their own time frame.

- Help the child learn about loss, grief and death so they can accept their feelings as normal and natural.
    - Share your feelings with them in an age-appropriate manner. Be aware that your extreme emotions can be frightening and should be dealt with elsewhere. However, having them see adults emote with tears in an honest and reasonable manner provides permission for them to release.
    - Give the gift of presence. Spend time, with or without talking.
    - Emphasize self-care (see "Self Care Relievers of Grief").
    - Encourage the release of feelings. Discuss helpful and hurtful ways to express feelings. Suggest the following ideas:
        - Physical activity of any kind. Join the child in the activity to show your support.
        - Allow a lot of time to play. In a child's world play is the natural outlet for feelings.
        - Create art through drawing, coloring, working with clay, etc. Great emotion may be released though art work and will give clues as to what a child may be feeling.
        - Write stories, poetry, letters and notes. This may prove to be of great relief to those who are not generally "talkers." Allow the child to keep the writings private if they wish.
        - Listen to music and watch movies with grief themes. These will bring emotions to the surface and provide a sense of connection. Examples are the movies "Wild Awake" and "Charlotte's Web."
    - Maintain structure and routine in the child's daily life. Rules provide safety. Use patience, kindness, and understanding, but do require the child to follow the rules of the home, school, and activities. It offers the stability they long for.
    - Provide opportunities to remember the loss. Talk about the person or place, share memories, make a memory book or memory box, plant a tree or bush, write letters to the person who is gone, etc. Children find comfort in remembering. Be aware of the sadness felt on holidays, anniversaries and/ or birthdays. Address how the child would like to commemorate the event.

For ease, the term "children" will denote ages 3-18 unless otherwise noted.

Stress Test*

Read each statement carefully, and then **check** a rating, depending on how often it applies to you <u>now</u>. There are no right or wrong answers. The more accurately you answer, the clearer you will be on where you need to improve your stress management.

Your Lifestyle	Almost Always	Often	Some-times	Occa-sionally	Almost Never
I eat at least one hot, balanced meal a day.					
I get seven to eight hours of sleep at least four nights a week.					
I give and receive affection regularly.					
I have at least one relative within 50 miles on whom I can rely.					
I exercise to the point of perspiration at least twice a week.					
I smoke less than half a pack of cigarettes a day (non-smokers score 1).					
I take fewer than five alcoholic drinks a week (non-drinkers score 1).					
I am the appropriate weight for my height.					
I have an income adequate to meet basic expenses.					
I get strength from my religious beliefs, or I feel comfortable with my view of the universe and my place in it.					
I regularly attend club or social activities.					
I have a network of friends/ acquaintances.					

Your Lifestyle	Almost Always	Often	Some-times	Occa-sionally	Almost Never
I have one or more friends to confide in about personal matters.					
I am in good health (including eyesight, hearing, teeth).					
I am able to speak openly about my feelings when angry or worried.					
I have regular conversations with the people I live with about domestic problems (ex., chores, money and daily living issues).					
I do something for fun at least once a week.					
I am able to organize my time effectively.					
I drink fewer than three cups of coffee (or tea or cola drinks) a day.					
I take quiet time for myself during the day.					
Total checks in each column					
Multiply by	x 1	x 2	x 3	x 4	x 5
Total for each column	+	+	+	+	=
Total for all columns =					

Total for all columns indicates:

Less than 50: Low vulnerability

50 - 70: Vulnerable to distress

70 - 95: Seriously vulnerable

More than 95: Extremely vulnerable

*Developed by Psychologists Lyle H. Miller and Alma Dell Smith at Boston University Medical Center

My Loss History

Schedule approximately one hour of quiet time to complete your loss history chart.

When completing your loss history, let your **feelings** about the losses be your guide. Each individual loss will bring a different intensity and response, depending on the event and when it occurred in your life. Be open and honest with yourself. Treat yourself with kindness about the discoveries you make.

1. **Begin by writing the following dates, memories, events across the line:**
   - Year of your birth
   - Your first memory: write in the year and note the memory
   - Midpoint of your life to date
   - Today's date
2. Take a few moments and ask yourself, "**What is the most painful or difficult loss I have ever experienced?**" Put the date of this loss on the horizontal line and draw a vertical line from that date to the bottom of the page. Make a small note on the vertical line to remind you of what loss the line represents.
3. Let your mind go back over your life and recall memories of other losses. Mark them on the line by placing the date above and drawing a vertical line downward, noting the loss. The length of the line will compare to the length of your most difficult loss (see #2).

Share your "My Loss History" with someone whom you feel is able to listen to you without judgment, questioning or trying to "fix you." Ask your listener to hear you with an open heart and a closed mouth. Ask the person not to touch you until you have completed talking about your loss history. If you cry, don't stop – keep talking while you cry. It is important to hear yourself confirm your feelings experiences. When you are finished, you may want to ask your listener to give you a big hug!

Reflect on what you have learned about yourself. Do not be judgmental. And thank yourself for being open to remembering and sharing.

If you are in need of a trusted listener, consider contacting your *Passages...through grief* leader, facilitator, or a pastor.

My Loss History

Birth

Mid-life

Today

Yeagley's
"Intentional Grieving"

Much of the grief I have observed during the last 22 years has been haphazard. People have been swept along by a flood of emotions, but like victims of a raging flash flood, they have had no choice in the matter. The emotions came over them instantly and furiously. When the initial fury briefly subsided, they tried to avoid further contact with the reminders of their loss. They hoped they could somehow escape any further contact with reality.

Edward is a case in point. He lost two children in the same disaster. Helplessly he went to work. Painfully he drove home in tears. He didn't know what to do to ease the pain, so he remained the victim of his grief that struck him with wavelike unpredictability. He was afraid to look at pictures of the children. Going into their bedroom was impossible.

"There must be something I can do to prevent grief from rendering me helpless at the most awkward times and places, but I don't know what it is," he said.

I shared with him an approach to grieving that occurred to me ten years ago. I have shared it with many people who found it extremely helpful. Let me share it with you.

Reserve a time slot for grieving each day. Pick a time when you will be undisturbed. Choose a place where you will feel free to talk aloud to yourself and cry. The length of this quiet time is up to you. Just make sure that you spend the time daily. Tell yourself that it is time for you to grieve. This takes away some of the haphazardness. You will begin to have a sense of control.

Provide some simple tools for your time of intentional grieving. You'll need a pencil, a notebook or journal, facial tissues, and a variety of objects that prompt memories such as portraits, snapshots, and trinkets, articles of clothing, jewelry, and letters. These items will change from time to time to correspond with the part of the relationship you are reconstructing.

At the beginning of each session choose one part of the relationship that used to be but can be no longer. For example, you may have gone fishing together. Think about all the fishing trips you can recall. Look at snapshots of fishing trips. Handle favorite lures and rods. Write some of the highlights of those trips in your notebook. Describe the feelings you had about the time together. Briefly record the happy times and the not-so-happy times. Jot down comments that the person made. Discipline yourself to focus only on your fishing adventures. If your mind wanders, simply tell yourself that you'll think about that later. Then go back to your work of reconstructing and reliving your fishing trips.

This exercise forces you to review the life of the person. Frequently people in grief can think of nothing but the death. It is therapeutic to evaluate the worth of a person's life and the worth of your relationship with that person.

The exercise also requires you to experience some pain that you'd normally dismiss from your mind in seconds. In your quiet time of intentional grieving, you face the pain longer. This allows the pain to lose its power to cut to the quick.

As you review one aspect of the relationship you will usually become aware that you will not experience it again in this life. This awareness is a crucial component of adjusting to your loss. Now is the time to confirm this reality.

In your notebook write a short farewell, read it aloud to yourself. Read it many times. You'll soon be able to say it without reading. Say it from your heart. The tears may come and the sobs may interrupt the flow of words. Don't attempt to stop the tears. Let them flow as you repeat the farewell. Keep repeating it until the sobbing subsides.

Your whole body will feel tense after many of your sessions. Lie on the floor face up. Tell yourself that your body is heavy and sinking through the floor. Breathe deeply and slowly. Remain in this relaxed position for at least ten minutes. Rise from the floor and end your time of intentional grieving by saying a simple prayer of thanks for the time you shared with that special person. You may want to create your own way of concluding each session.

Intentional grieving times focus the emotions that might otherwise become vague or blurred. When the emotions are tied to one aspect of the relationship, you are more likely to notice movement in your adjustment to your loss. Movement is the goal, not time. Don't concern yourself with how long grief lasts. Watch for movement toward adjustment. Intentional grieving sessions can prevent getting stuck in some part of the grieving process.

I have noticed that men appreciate this approach because men like to fix things and take charge. This organized method gives them some control, something they can do about grief. They see progress even though it is in small increments.

Even though an increasing number of men have been attending bereavement support groups, many men still believe they can grieve on their own. Quiet and regular sessions in the privacy of the home, following a simple procedure, give men a constructive alternative to attending a group or keeping busy to forget.

Ideally a grieving person should have at least one support person with whom he or she can talk. Keeping a notebook or journal during intentional grieving sessions provides a good source of discussion when sharing with a support person. I encourage people to bring their written material to their sessions with me. It is especially helpful to read farewells to another person.

Your written material is an excellent resource for helping you determine whether you are moving toward adjustment. This is done by periodically reading your journal from the beginning. If your reading triggers less pain, you will know that you have made progress. The general content will also reveal movement.

A nurse gave me permission to use her journal to illustrate how intentional grieving promotes movement toward adjustment.

Five weeks after her husband died she wrote, "I'm beginning to know you're really gone. NO, I don't really believe you're gone yet. Not yet!"

Two months after her loss she wrote, "I feel such loneliness and sadness, but the terrible anguish I felt the first weeks is slowly easing up. I try now to think of ways to live without you. I pray for strength to go on."

Three months after the death she wrote, "I think today was the turning point. I think I'm beginning to accept your death. It's final. Tonight I'm calm. No tears tonight. I miss you. I wish you were beside me to kiss me goodnight. Never again though will you do that, nor will I be able to touch you or say I love you except to your picture or your memory."

At the end of the fifth month she wrote, "Tomorrow is our anniversary – 34 years. I've had a good day. Don't know if it's because I've been so busy or if God's answered my prayer for peace."

After six months she wrote, "I think I've entered a new phase of this grief. It's reality now. You've gone forever and I'm alive. I want to be alive. I want to enjoy living again."

These few excerpts from her journal reveal a movement toward life without her husband. As I reviewed the journal with her, she marveled at the progress she had made in six months. Much of that was due to her willingness to grieve intentionally.

Yeagley's

Be Good to Yourself

When great losses come to us, we sometimes feel that there is no use going on. Our self-esteem is greatly diminished. We see no reason to take care of ourselves because we are worthless - or so we think.

I frequently meet people in grief who have become so convinced of their worthlessness that they eat poorly, dress in poor taste, and practice grooming habits far inferior to their usual standards. Almost total immobilization sets in. Rarely do they go out of the house. Newspapers, books and magazines of interest go untouched.

If this is happening to you, make a careful study of the fifteenth chapter of the Gospel According to Luke. The key lesson of the three stories in that chapter is that God places an enormous amount of value on each person, even when we are very disappointed with our own failures. We may feel worthless and rejected, but our value in God's sight has not changed. This is very important for a grieving person to understand.

Move another step toward the realization that your potential for loving others and living creatively still exists. The object of your love may be gone so that there is no love given in response to yours, but your potential for loving is the same. Love is of God. The source of love has not dried up. Your potential for living creatively is unchanged. The person who shared in much of your creativity is gone, but creativity only waits to be shared with others.

You still have life. Life is a gift that cannot tolerate being kept in a box. It must be shared for the benefit of others if it's to thrive.

If you decide to withdraw from others and live in the past for the rest of your life, you are only hurting yourself more than you are already hurt. Healing comes by reaching out and using the beautiful commodity – your God-given life.

Be good to yourself and move out into life. Not too fast at first, you understand. Move out a step at a time. It's possible to move out of the circle of grief prematurely. One way of knowing if you're doing this is when every little action requires force on your part and you're extremely exhausted.

Some women take little steps like making a pie "from scratch" instead of taking one from the freezer, or writing a letter to a person who needs to be encouraged. Some men go to the hardware store for supplies and then fix a leaky faucet, or they may wash and wax the car.

Be good to yourself by getting a good physical examination. When the doctor gives you his assessment, ask him what kind of exercise would be suitable for you. Keep the exercise program interesting and within your physical limits, but, whatever you do, keep active.

Grief has a way of tightening up the muscles of your body so that you don't breathe deeply. This tightening can be eliminated by proper exercise. Perhaps a vigorous walk concluded by a leisurely stroll of equal length would be ideal for most people.

Death and divorce are the greatest stressors to the human system. They bring changes that require many adjustments. To add more change on top of one of these major changes is asking for real trouble. As much as possible, avoid changes for the first year or so. Your adjustment to a major loss will be much easier if you can keep all of the other areas of life stable.

Friends and family may advise you to sell the house, change jobs, move away, or have somebody come and live with you, but this is not the best advice in most cases. If circumstances are such that these changes are necessary, fine. In most cases it is wise to wait until you have been able to resolve the grief.

Stress is unavoidable. The days following the loss will bring their conflict. Learning how to handle conflict is important. Let me share a few ideas.

- When conflict arises, don't act on a whim. Slow down. Pray to God for wisdom and perspective.
- Talk with a friend who can help you discover the origin of your conflict.
- Think it through very carefully. This can be done by listing all the possible options and the possible results of following each of these options.
- Choose one or two options that you feel are the best and do what you can about them. Be careful to do what can be done today, today, and put off what can't be done until tomorrow for tomorrow, and forget about that which is out of your control.

These four tips help when the crisis comes, but improving your coping skills is a long-range project. I like to call our coping ability our cool range. It is something like a temperature gauge on a car. Below a certain point is freeze-up. Above a certain point is boil-over.

This cool range can be narrowed by our lifestyle. Grief is the greatest pressure that narrows the cool range. When we experience grief we must be on guard against a host of other conditions that further narrow the range. Among these are fear, anger, discouragement, jealousy, envy, resentment, sedentary lifestyle, violence, excessive change, domestic strife, pressure to achieve, boredom, smoking, drugs, breakfast skipping, poor nutrition, under-rest, overwork and alcohol.

On the positive side there are simple, yet effective measures we can take to broaden our cool range. Among these are the expression of gratitude to God and to mankind, the expression of affection, joy, forgiveness, courage, hope, peace and trust in God, an exercise program that suits our health, a good relaxation program, and good health habits.

As we're going through grief the pressures of life still keep coming at us. In fact, business matters related to settling estates or negotiating with insurance companies increase the things that cry for our attention. One woman told me, "I never knew my husband had business dealings with half of the people who are pushing for settlement."

It's helpful to think of our minds as filters. We decide which of the items coming at us will be labeled "discard," "unimportant," "can wait, "vital," or "top priority." Only a few items filter through as necessary in a given day.

I'm actually advocating that people in grief must be good to themselves by simplifying life each day. If someone has to wait a few more days or weeks because of your grief – so what? Grief is no picnic. You deserve a little pampering.

Shortly after our son died, friends took us to a Pennsylvania Dutch smorgasbord. They had also lost a child and probably sensed that we needed a special treat. We would not have done it on our own because we were numbed by our grief. Fourteen years later we stopped at the same restaurant. I reflected on how beneficial it was to have a change of scenery.

My personal way of being good to myself is to plan time for creative solitude. I tied my canoe to my car and headed for a dam 50 miles from home. I took a lunch and a thermos of hot chocolate. I paddled to the dam breast and pointed the canoe toward the opposite end. The wind was at my back so I lay down in the canoe and propped my head up on a cushion. As the wind pushed my craft I slept. At the end of the dam I was awakened by the waves lapping against the canoe and the noisy red-winged blackbirds protecting their nests. I ate lunch and then paddled upwind to my car. Because it was late October there wasn't another person at the dam. It was my world and my time for stretching my spiritual muscles.

I visited a woman who had lost her husband a year earlier. She had closed up her house and refused to answer her phone. In her reclusive state she had become depressed and physically frail. I immediately made my way to her front parlor. Through the large picture window I gazed at the large lake dotted with sailboats. The stimulating resort town lay before her, but she was a prisoner because she had chosen to suffer. For an hour I challenged her to be good to herself. I told her that there is a time to grieve, but there must also be a time to let people, places and things draw us away from our pain.

A widow in Texas found a fascinating way to be good to herself. On Thanksgiving and Christmas she served dinner to hundreds of people. A philanthropist financed the meals in the large city of Fort Worth, Texas. Some of the guests were homeless, some were friendless and some were sickly, but all were welcomed into the warmth of a large banquet hall. The Texas widow brought them food, hugged them, laughed with them and sang with them. Without realizing it, she had done herself a greater favor.

Yes, I know you don't feel like doing yourself a favor, but do it anyway. You deserve it. You are special.

Reflection Time

Complete after *Passages...through grief* session

Date: _____

What event or experience had an impact on you at the session tonight?

What feelings, thoughts, or insights did you notice?

What was helpful?

What were your feeling(s) in the closing circle?

Reflection Time

Date: _____

Think about your day today. What is a feeling you have felt (use **Feelings Chart** if help is needed for recognition)?

What event or experience had an impact on you?

What have you done for yourself?

Your thoughts or reactions:

Session Four

Session Four Information for Leaders

Passages Foundations (45-50 minutes)

Welcome
Moment of silence to recognize their courage
Discussion of **My Loss History** p. 130

- Ask for questions or concerns
- Did any losses surprise them?
- Ask participants to note incomplete losses
    o   Refer to **Cleaning Out the Closet** p. 13
    o   Refer to **Wound Concept** p. 14

Leader shares personal grief story and chart for **Charting Our Relationship**

- Refer to **Charting Our Relationship** p. 142 (PM p. 89)
- Refer to Charting Our Relationship sample p. 143

Introduce **Charting Our Relationship** pp. 145-146 (PM pp. 89-90)

- Ask participants to select a loss to use, either the present or another unfinished loss
- Begin filling in their chart in group (5 minutes)

Read aloud **Grief is...** p. 147 (PM p. 91)

- Ask for clarification of understanding

Review **Intentional Grieving** p. 151 (PM p. 95)

- Draw attention to the elements that facilitate intentional grieving as found in Yeagley's "Intentional Grieving" p. 131 (PM p. 73)
- Complete questions at the end of the article (5 minutes)

Discuss **Anger - What Can I do About It?** p. 149 (PM p. 93)

- Ask for means of release they have found helpful

Break (5 – 10 minutes)

At end of break, each facilitator gathers their sharing group members and moves to their meeting space

- Facilitators take the **Affirmation** poster

Sharing Group(s) (45 minutes)

Read aloud together the **Affirmation** poster
If the group needs guidance, offer the following questions:

- Are they recognizing their own grief as a process?
- Are they sharing their grief experience?
- What skills are they developing?

In Closing (15 minutes)

Invite them to bring a **memento** next week (e.g. pictures, cards, trinkets)
Draw attention to **Follow-up for the Week**, especially **Charting the Relationship**
Mark calendars to meet 30 minutes early for Session Six to share a meal
Closing Ritual—gather participants into a circle and invite them to "Name a feeling you've felt tonight."

- Leader invites participants to join hands and close eyes.
- Leader begins by stating a feeling
- Conclude with "Go in peace."

Post Session Meeting for Leaders and Facilitators

Review and discuss:

- The overall functioning of the whole and sharing groups
- Prepare weekly letters for each participant
    o Arrange for mailing

Enjoy each other!

Charting Our Relationship

The second of the trilogy of decisive grief assignments is "Charting Our Relationship." *
In this piece each participant selects one of the losses from "My Loss History" to examine
for the memories that had an impact, either positive or negative. The participants assign
the length of the line depending on the intensity of the event (both positive and negative)
at the time it happened. From this timeline, facets emerge that have left the griever
incomplete in their resolution of the relationship.

Visualizing the charted recollections across time brings the participant into closer
contact with their memories and the person. The unresolved issues and regrets become
more apparent. It is as if the participant creates their own confrontation with what has
been left behind. It is understandable that the exercise is challenging. However, it is very
important for the leader to encourage the group members to take on this challenge as
a key in their healing steps. It is also valuable to have this work done prior to the next
week's assignment, as the material they produce with "Charting Our Relationship" is used
directly in the final project.

This model can be used in working on the present grief or another unfinished loss. We
have found that in pointing this out to participants, they are generally relieved to have
something concrete that can be useful to address the other incomplete losses that have
surfaced.

*A sample of "Charting Our Relationship" follows from one of the original leaders. Feel
free to use the story and the chart to make your own for your program.

1. In the sample the leader begins by stating:

"I'm going to tell you about a relationship I needed to focus on in my own life.
"For my first two plus decades, Dad was the most powerful person in my life. He was a
complex person...giving and controlling, flawed and tender. He was a preacher, a gardener,
a golfer and not much of a family man. I admired him. I feared him. I loved him. I hated
him. I longed for his approval and demonstrations of his love for me and our family. He
was great in a crisis...grounded and present to one's needs. My father.
"In considering our relationship over the years, I created a graph of specific events...
ongoing scenarios and enduring traits that had an impact on my life with him and our
relationship."

**2. The leader exhibits the relationship chart she/he has created, pointing to a few
events or traits as illustrations.**

Charting Our Relationship Sample

My relationship with my father

Beginning

discipline- switchings

teasing and games

tonsils

garden master

tender Christmas moments

"tone of voice"

went to counselor with me in 2nd year of college

married us

could not apologize

unkind granddad to my children

stood up to him

long conversations

needing to be the center of attention

his death

Today

Session Four Guide for Participants

Follow-up for the Week:

Complete *Charting Our Relationship* graph
Review *Small Steps*
Read Yeagley's articles:
    "Moving Toward Recovery"
    "Review and Reconstruction"
    "What is Saying Goodbye?"
Use *Reflection Time* notes to support your writing for the week
Bring a memento next week!
Mark your calendars to meet at 6:30 for our final session (in two weeks) for a Pot-Luck Dinner. (Optional)

Charting Our Relationship

_____ *(name)*

"Charting Our Relationship" is a useful tool to help you process losses
which have left you feeling unfinished or incomplete.

- On "My Loss History" read through your losses and note those that are unfinished for you. To decide what these are, consider where there is still unresolved conflict, the inability to say what you wish you had said, or if the loss remains very painful. Be honest with yourself. Recognize that this is about your reaction and not about the other person.
- Choose one loss—the one that is most painful and difficult for you at present. Or if too painful, choose a loss you **can** work with at this time.
- Focusing on this one loss, use "Charting Our Relationship" (see next page) to reconstruct the relationship. Think of your memories, both positive and negative, and the misunderstandings. Do not limit or edit your memories. Just remember and write them down.
- Think of the most positive memory you have. Note it at the top of the sheet. Then draw a vertical line to the horizontal line. **All positive memories, experiences and processes are marked above the horizontal line.** The length of the line will depend on the power of your feelings at the time the event/experience occurred.
- **Negative memories, experiences and processes * are marked below the horizontal line.** The length of the line will depend on the power of your feelings about the event/experience/process. The longest line will be the most negative recall with that person.

* An example of a negative process would be recalling painful teasing or verbal abuse that occurred chronically.

Charting Our Relationship Graph

My relationship with _____

Beginning _____ Today

Grief is...

As we have discussed, there are various difficult and powerful feeling experiences that may well surface during the grieving process. Some we expect, like sadness, lost-ness or tenderness. However, when anger or guilt surface, we may have a hard time identifying and tolerating them, or knowing just how to deal with them.

ANGER

Let's begin with **anger**. Anger brings up powerful, negative energy. Think of it as spiking a fever when there is an infection. Anger, like the fever, is signaling that **something is wrong!** It is normal and healthy to get a fever as a signal, and it is normal and healthy to get angry at times—nothing bad about that. The key is to notice the anger and begin to search for the source or target of the anger, and then figure out what needs to be done to relieve it.

If one starts to feel angry and then tries to push the feelings down, it gets turned in on the self and will find other outlets. This is called **internalized anger**. Often it expresses itself in depression or illnesses such as ulcers, colitis or headaches. On the other hand, **externalized** anger refers to using outward expressions of anger, from body language and facial expressions to aggressive behavior. A person might target others who are not really the source of the anger, but are "safe" enough to "dump on." Verbal or emotional abuse, kicking the dog, or road rage are examples of what is called **displaced anger**. This, of course, damages relationships and others without resolving the angry feelings. Further, anger that is unfinished may lead to emotional issues.

Clinical depression refers to a mental illness people are worried about having. The symptoms of depression are loss of energy, interest; sadness, sleep disturbance, eating disturbance; diminished ability to think or concentrate; thoughts of death. People experiencing grief often experience these symptoms. The difference is that grievers can point to the specific, significant loss or change precipitating the reaction. And with intentional grief work, the symptoms usually fade. If, however, symptoms continue to be of concern, one should consult a professional so that a combination of talk therapy and medication may be used to work through the grief-induced depression.

GUILT

Guilt is another difficult feeling that may surface during grief that needs to be identified and dealt with directly. First, guilt and regret need to be differentiated. There are instances of **regret** in most relationships or roles—times when we have done something we wish we had not, or times when we have not done what we would have liked. Regrets. Little losses in themselves. **Guilt** is a different matter. It is appropriate to feel guilty when a person has intentionally injured or actually hurt another unintentionally. When we have actively wronged someone and we could be prosecuted, it is appropriate to feel realistic guilt. For most, that is not the way guilt works. **We feel guilty for situations where regret is more fitting**. And guilt, operating as it does, tends to grow and spread. In short, feeling guilty we tend to focus more and more on ourselves, our shortcomings, our "terribleness," and lose track of the other person, and how we might make amends. Ultimately, this cycle of personal fault-finding, known as "feeling guilty," doesn't help anyone and is unhealthy.

Anger – What Can I do About It?

Anger is a normal and natural reaction. All people have anger; not all will allow themselves to recognize it. Anger, if left unchecked, can cause great emotional and physical stress. It is powerful.

Think about your anger...

What are you angry about?
Focus on the specific cause: "I am angry at..." or "I am angry because..."
Are you really angry at a person or are you misdirecting the anger onto someone else?
We often misdirect our anger because it's easier. However this creates problems with others who may not deserve our anger. Look for the true source.
What is your anger telling you?
What need is not being fulfilled? What is incomplete? What needs to be different?
How does your anger feel?
It's inside of you. Try to describe how it is affecting you. How big is it? In what part of your body does it reside? What does the anger do there?
What does your anger look like?
If you were to draw your anger, how would it look on the page? What color is it? What number value would you assign its intensity?

Once anger is acknowledged, it can begin to dissipate.
Ways to release anger:

- Talk with someone who is willing to listen without judgment. Choose a person who will listen without making comments or criticism about your angry feelings. If no one comes to mind, talk with a counselor, clergy person or a **Passages...through grief** leader. It is valuable to hear your words voiced.
- Use the "Reflection Time" sheets
- Release stress through physical exercise
- Take opportunities to intentionally release your anger (see article on "Intentional Grieving"). Suggestions include:
    o Garden—yank up the weeds!
    o Yell or scream; use a pillow to absorb the noise; go in the bathroom with the water running; sing or yell while in a car (preferably when it's parked!)

- o Hit something—
  - Use your pillow to beat your mattress, sofa, chairs
  - Use a bat to hit a tree
  - Pound nails into a piece of wood
  - Use a punching bag
  - Hit ice cubes with a bat or golf club
- o Throw—
  - Bean bags
  - Eggs - write your angry feelings on them and throw them at a tree
  - China – buy cheap pieces and throw them at a wall
  - Tennis balls
- o Knead bread
- o Rip up an old phone book
- For the future, you may use the energy of your anger to start or join a program that is constructive—
  - o Work to change laws
  - o Gather people in the name of a cause that will deal with the unfairness of what has happened to you
  - o Look inside yourself to find your calling

Intentional Grieving

Grieving intentionally means allowing a specific time and space where the memories and feelings can surface and be dealt with in the present. We can think of it as allowing space for completing an aspect of the loss. There's no one "right way" to grieve intentionally, though there are common elements usually present. The Yeagley reading "Intentional Grieving" from Session Three suggests the following elements:

- o a quiet space
- o a regular, undisturbed time
- o tissues, candles, memory-makers (ex., photos, old letters)
- o reflection paper, pen/pencil
- o a willingness to experience one aspect of the loss
- o determination to stay focused on **one aspect**
- o gentle self-care

Use of these elements will not only offer the opportunity to release associated pain, but will also encourage "the self" in knowing you can be trusted to manage your very tenderness. This second part is vital in healing, for the very core of our self longs to be made whole. And when we allow time, patience, and follow-through with grief episodes, the self recognizes this as our strength and reliability, and ushers forth what needs healing.

If one has been used to avoiding difficult feelings, it will take patience and time for the self to get the new message of the desire to heal and your availability to experience the process. This may well sound quite simple. And it is SIMPLE. But at the same time, it is truly difficult. "Difficult" is the term, especially when beginning intentional grief. Fears occur of never-ending tears or pain, or of not being able to experience life with joy. However, as time with the process progresses, you will find that it becomes less difficult and more normal and natural. Having times with yourself, where you are actively taking care of yourself and your deep longings, builds confidence. This is very healthy but may feel awkward for a while, like wearing a new pair of shoes.

What has been described here is the process of <u>letting go</u> - not of the person, but the releasing of what is no longer possible to experience in this life. And what we let go of is the attachment, and the pain and fear of detaching. When letting go occurs, feelings calm and pain diminishes, leaving the memories we choose to carry forward. Take a moment to recall something you have had to let go of in the past, something or some relationship you were able to release, and note it here_____

At this time, what are other situations you want to be able to release?

_____
_____
_____
_____

Yeagley's

"Moving Toward Recovery"

When a person goes through grief, he or she is caught between the need to suffer pain and the urge to run.

The sooner and the more intensely the person experiences suffering, the sooner he recovers. I must qualify that statement however. When a person experiences great change in life through death or divorce, and then suffers pain in coming to terms with the change, there can be either growth or devastation as a result. When change and pain are accompanied by the support of meaningfully-related people, there is growth. Deprived of support, a person can become very bitter.

For this reason a grieving person should be encouraged to reach out to others and to lean on friends and professional helpers.

Running puts off the experience of pain to a later time. Ways of running are legion. Drink, drugs, travel, work, promiscuity, reckless sports, and pleasure extravaganzas are just a few. The tragedy of running is the devastation and heartache that so often occur. Ultimately a person must go through the pain in order to be healed. How much better it is to let the pain happen early in grief.

I will suggest four steps that are certain to move you toward recovery:

Think

This may be the opposite of some of the advice given to you. Frequently people are told, "Just put it out of your mind. Don't think about it. Stay away from the place where he lived. Don't go near the cemetery where you are forced to think about him."

I would encourage you to be unafraid of your thoughts. Let them happen. For instance, if you drive by the restaurant where you had dinner with the person, relive the entire evening in your mind. Recall the menu, the conversation, how he was dressed, and the ride home.

If you live in the house where the person resided before death, go from room to room and rethink all of the events connected with each room. The room where you had eaten your first meal after the honeymoon, the room where you listened to your favorite music, the room where the children were conceived, the room where you last kissed - take a memory trip through familiar places.

The thinking process helps us to accept the reality of the loss both intellectually and emotionally. Intellectual acceptance comes easily, but emotional acceptance doesn't come until some months after the loss.

In driver's education we learn that there is some distance between the time when we apply the brakes and the time when the car stops. The application of death or divorce news may register in the head almost immediately, but the registering in the heart, like the full stopping of the car, is some time away.

The thinking process facilitates acceptance.

Write

You can think thirty years in three minutes, but it takes longer to write it. That's why I suggest that grieving people keep a journal during their grief. Write down all the details, but also the feelings you have. Tell your journal how life is different without the person you lost. Tell about the things that help and that hurt. Analyze your anger, your loneliness, and your frustration. Be very open with your journal. This slows down your thinking and tends to lessen the pain that accompanied your first thoughts.

Talk

Talk to people who are willing to listen without feeling they need to say something. Choose a person who isn't judgmental.

Have a certain progression to your talking. Starting with the immediate loss, talk about details and feelings concerning events all the way back to the first time you met the person who died. If the relationship with the person you are talking to permits, talk about all the relationships with other people prior to your meeting the person who died. Reviewing meaningful relationships prior to meeting the deceased will help you to accept the possibility of having meaningful relationships after the death.

Talking is a process whereby you gradually experience a lessening of the acute pain of separation. You begin to say good-bye, to psychologically emancipate yourself from the bondage you willingly formed with the person who died.

Gradually change the thrust of your conversation to yourself and your future, but first of all, be sure you have spoken about your grief feelings as extensively as you need to.

Weep

Weeping is a God-given release when we are going through a time of stress. Do not choke back the tears. Let them flow. Crying is not an indication of a weakened faith. The New Testament indicated that Jesus wept. Why shouldn't we?

I spoke to a group of 35 Methodist women about grief. All of them were weeping at the same time. I commented, "I'm happy to see that all of you are healthy." They were amused at my comment, but I was really serious. Weeping during grief is healthy.

Dr. James Peterson of the University of Southern California says, "No one cries very much unless something of real worth is lost. So grieving is a celebration of the depth of the union. Tears are the jewels of remembrance—sad, but glistening with the beauty of the past." ("On Being Along" The Adventist Chaplain, Nov. 1975, Glendale, CA p.5)

The four steps are in no way seen as a magic cure. They are simply facilitators of the grief process. Grief is not resolved in a hurry. Most people want to know how long grief lasts, but there is no way of putting a time on it. Some authors say that acute grief lasts 6 to 8 months. Don't count on it. Instead of keeping track of the months, look for subtle improvements. Rejoice over each small advancement. You'll take a few steps backward, but that's to be expected. As long as you keep your eyes on the goal, you'll do fine.

Speaking of healing, C.S. Lewis said, "There was no sudden, striking and emotional transition. Like the warming of a room or the coming of daylight, when you first notice them they have already been going on for some time." (*A Grief Observed*, The Seabury Press, 1963, p.49)

As I write this chapter I look back over 18 years of conducting bereavement support groups. I recommended the four steps to each group because they really help to resolve the difficult issues every grieving person faces. A person in grief is often in a listless state and can spend months doing nothing to adjust. Such a person may feel very much out of control, but these steps restore a sense of being in control.

I have observed that feelings of anxiety are less when people have some choices in how grief proceeds. That's why I tell them to set a time each day for thinking, writing, talking and crying. This deliberate grieving reduces the times of breaking down in public.

If you avoid active grief, you may think you are handling your loss, but there may be little forward motion. You have to go through the pain produced by these four steps if you want to adjust to your loss.

Yeagley's

"Review and Reconstruction"

Frequently I am with families in the emergency room when the physician announces the death of a loved one. The reactions vary. The usual response is stabbing pain followed by tears. Within minutes a numbing effect takes over. Sometimes short periods of rage appear, but regardless, disbelief settles in. Even after seeing the body, the family walk to their cars saying, "I just can't believe it. This can't be happening to us."

The funeral is usually a blur. The family knows there were many people there, but they can't remember names. The minister's remarks are seldom remembered. The whole episode seems like a bad dream.

Soon after the funeral many people go in search of the person who died. They look for the lost in crowds, at church, on subways and at home. They pine and yearn for the person to be there as usual.

A friend of mine was completing a house that he and his wife started to build just before she died. Seven months after her death he said to me, "I have never admitted this to a soul, but I really do believe that when I move into that house she'll be there."

A woman told me that she fully expects to see her husband in his usual chair when she gets home from grocery shopping. When he isn't there she goes about the house calling his name. He never answers. After the letdown she curls up on the bed and cries.

These are not unusual behaviors. Intellectually, the reality has registered to some degree. On all other levels the person still lives with the loved one.

In early grief a person strives to keep the relationship alive. Great efforts are made to retain the sense of presence, but underlying these efforts is the sad awareness that all efforts are futile.

In my early work with grieving people I urged them to say good-bye to their relationship with the lost. Many of these people resisted my suggestion because they were still searching for the person who was missing. They were putting all their energy into preserving the relationship...the opposite of what I was asking them to do.

Pamela came to my office on several occasions. She listened to me saying, "Pamela, it might be helpful if you could say good-bye to your relationship with Jack. You are trying to hold on to someone who is no longer able to meet your needs."

One day she turned to me and screamed, "I don't want to say good-bye to Jack. Can't you understand? I want him with me and you won't take him away from me."

Pamela and many other grieving friends of mine have concluded that it's better to cooperate with the early need to cling to the relationship than to resist it.

They discover that reviewing and reconstructing the total relationship has a comforting quality. Not only is it comforting, it also gets the expression of feelings started. This wards off getting stuck midstream in grief.

As people share their recollections of a relationship with me, they'll sometimes stare out the window. With a smile on their faces they'll say something like, "I'll never forget how happy we were when we were married. Ben was full of life. So handsome. And I was so proud to be in his arms."

Sometimes there is laughter as we review a part of the relationship. The laughter relaxes tense muscles. Laughter is also a way of expressing sorrow when tears do not come easily.

After weeks of thinking, journaling and talking about her husband, a woman had an amazing breakthrough. It happened after an hour of reminiscing and laughing about the humorous qualities of their relationship. For the first time since her husband died, she was smiling. That smile went to the very depths of her soul. She said to herself, "Ah, I can feel well again. This is a sign that I'll find life worth living even though my husband died. This must be an evidence of healing."

This is exactly what I wanted her to discover in her early grief. This discovery took place by following her natural attempts to keep the relationship alive. By early review and reconstruction, she moved to a point where she was ready to begin saying good-bye. That couldn't happen until she had a small promise of healing on the horizon.

Hospital staff need to see the important role they play in this process. They are often with people at the time of death. A physician, nurse, social worker or chaplain can encourage the newly bereaved family to tell the story of the person's life. Reviewing can begin immediately, if hospital staff will take time to be with the family.

When a loved one dies, the bereaved person wants to share with another person how worthwhile the loved one was. When that opportunity is not provided, there is an empty feeling inside. A choked up sensation takes over, making future sharing of feelings difficult.

Reviewing and reconstructing the relationship becomes repetitive. People say to me, "I must sound like a broken record. Aren't you bored with this?"

I am very quick to let them know that the repetition is vital. How I feel isn't important. What the repetition is doing for them is what really matters.

Grieving people must find a tolerant and non-judgmental friend who will listen patiently. They need people who will share their story many times.

People who don't understand the value of reviewing say things like, "You've got to quit going over the same thing again and again. It's not doing you a bit of good." But it is doing good.

Frequently, reviewing the relationship will bring some unpleasant things to the surface. This is a necessary part of therapy.

A widow was talking about how protective her husband was. He cared for everything. She didn't even know how to write a check. She suddenly blurted out, "Why didn't Danny teach me some of these things? He babied me too much. Maybe if he hadn't made me so dependent, I could handle being alone."

A divorced man told his story for the fifth time. He said, "She was always so passive. I wish she had spoken up and told me what was eating at her, then I could have done something to change. Now I know what I needed to change, but she won't give me a chance."

Talking about the negative parts of the relationship provides a chance to admit anger and analyze it constructively. Admission of guilt also takes place. Once these feelings are confronted they can be analyzed and resolved.

Part of the relationship that needs to be verbalized is the series of events that led up to the death and the death itself. In the case of divorce, the series of events leading up to the separation needs to be put into words. These painful events can be locked in the mind and never be discussed. This is a mistake. Reviewing these events with others mellows the pain.

Any part of the relationship that a person wishes to avoid should be reviewed and reconstructed deliberately. The longer avoidance is practiced, the more difficult adjustment will be.

One of my favorite ways of helping a grieving person is to sit back in my chair and say, "John must have been a unique person in your life. Tell me about him." Then I listen as long as the person cares to talk.

Scores of people finish a session like this by saying, "I feel so much better now that I've talked about him. I guess I needed to do it."

Separation from a loved one is unnatural to the mind. The cutting short of a relationship may be irreversible, but the lingering afterglow need not be denied. Totally experiencing that warmth is both comforting and preparatory to recovery.

Don't force yourself to review and reconstruct the entire relationship in one sitting. You'll tire yourself. Too much at one time may produce anxiety. Go about it slowly. Give yourself weeks or months to cover the relationship in depth.

Some days you may feel like taking a break from thinking about the past. You probably need a respite from the pain. Go ahead and occupy yourself with diversionary activity. After all, emotions are similar to the muscles of your body. Both are meant to be relaxed periodically.

As you reminisce over the past you will gradually admit to yourself that experiences with the person will not happen again. Slowly you will sense the need to bid farewell to what cannot be.

Yeagley's

"What is Saying Goodbye?"

My decision to leave home at sixteen to attend private school was exciting. The lure of the big city made me eager to be on my way. I loaded my foot locker into the trunk of the 1942 Studebaker. My father made sure the barnyard gate was closed and then he climbed behind the wheel. As we drove down the lane, strange feelings began to churn inside. The feelings became stronger as we carried the footlocker into the rooming house in downtown Philadelphia. It was all so foreign to me.

In the school parking lot I bid my parents farewell. My mother hugged me for the first time that I could remember. My father awkwardly hugged me. The only other physical contacts with my father were an occasional good-natured slap on the knee as we worked together and an occasional spanking.

They drove out of the parking lot. There I stood...all alone in a new world. The confusing feelings that had built up during the three-hour trip suddenly burned their way to my tear ducts. I fought the tears back, but to no avail. The old Studebaker looked blurred as it disappeared down Drexel Road. The lump in my throat was so big that I feared choking.

I walked around the corner of the school where nobody could see me. There I regained my composure before facing my new school family.

Saying goodbye was the most painful experience of my life up to that time. Even though I would have both of my parents for thirty years more, that first good-bye was a shattering experience.

With the passing of years I have had to say good-bye to relationships that were terminated by death. The pain of knowing that there would be no more reunions in this life nearly paralyzed me. Many times I wondered how I could go on, but I did go on. I did say good-bye. I did find healing.

I learned how to say good-bye from the scores of grieving people who have come into my life in the last twenty-five years. I'll share their secrets in this chapter.

Reviewing and reconstructing the relationship in thought, journaling and conversation is essential to saying good-bye. Celebration of relationship precedes termination of relationship.

When I tell people they need to say good-bye, they cringe because they misunderstand.

I don't advocate saying good-bye to memories. Memories are the priceless gems securely encased in the mind.

I conducted a seminar for sixteen people. The average age was 82. Ella stood out in bold relief. She was 86. She began telling her story. "My dear husband died in this very hospital just two weeks ago," she said in a quivering voice. "I can't tell you what a blow it has been to me."

Struggling with tears she continued. "But I've got to get hold of myself. I've got to put him out of my mind. I can't think about him. I've got to try not to think about him."

"Ella, do you have any children?" I asked.

"Yes, sir. I have two sons," she informed me proudly.

"Do you remember when your oldest son went to school the first day?"

"Yes."

"Now, Ella, I want you to pretend. Pretend that you're standing at the front door of your house on that first school day. You stoop down and say, 'Willie, when you go past old Mr. York's cherry tree, don't you dare think about red-eyed elephants in the cherry tree.' You tell him that three times before he leaves the house. You warn him again as he leaves the front yard.'

"Now tell me, Ella. What is Willie going to think about when he passes Mr. York's cherry tree?"

A slight twinkle came into her eyes as she said, "Why, the red-eyed elephants, of course."

"And when they told you not to think about your husband, what did you think about?" I asked.

"My husband. After all, we lived together for nearly 60 years. How could I not think about him?" she responded.

"Ella, you have my permission to go back over your wonderful memories of your husband. I'd love to hear about how you met him. I like romance stories. Could you share with me?" I eagerly asked.

That was just the invitation she needed. For twenty minutes Ella shared her memories with us. At certain points she was laughing through her tears.

She finally gave a loud sigh and exclaimed, "Oh, I feel so much better now. I wish somebody had told me two weeks ago that it was alright to remember."

Memories are painful at first, but with adjustment they are monuments to the worthwhileness of that person's life.

I don't ask a grieving individual to say good-bye to the person. The unique character and personality of the loved one is integrally woven into the life-fabric of the person who grieves. To say good-bye to the person would require removing many elements of one's lifestyle that are irreversibly stamped by the influence of that person.

Parents who lose a child and try to say good-bye to that person are in for painful surprises. One day they may hear or see the identical expressions and mannerisms of the dead child in one of their living children.

I have met parents who avoided a living child because he or she reminded them of the child who died.

Saying good-bye to the person is not realistic...to say the least.

Saying good-bye to hopes of meeting the person who died is never encouraged. In my experience with grieving people, I have concluded that this hope facilitates the desired recovery. When a person has no hope of ever seeing his or her loved one again, the journey toward adjustment is much rockier.

To rip that hope away from a person is inexcusable. Therapists who insist that a grieving person say good-bye "forever" or that he or she will "never" see the loved one again are not wise.

A clinical psychologist friend of mine came to be with me in a time of loss. He put his hand on my shoulder, looked into my eyes and said, "Larry, now what do you think of the scant empirical studies that suggest faith doesn't really make a difference?"

My response was immediate. "I think they need to do more thorough research."

"I agree with you one hundred percent," he replied. I knew by his tone of voice that hope had guided him through a deep loss.

If I don't ask people to say good-bye to memories, the person, or their hopes of future reunion, what do I encourage them to say good-bye to? I encourage them to say good-bye to the relationship as it once existed but can no longer exist in this lifetime.

When a grieving person reaches out to a relationship that has ceased, the absence of response is frustrating. Human needs, once met by that relationship, are no longer met. Anxiety mounts. Loneliness deepens. Depression settles in.

These unpleasant experiences could last over a long period. They could cause you to get stuck in grief. To prevent this I suggest saying good-by to the relationship in bits and pieces.

If a person has already reviewed and reconstructed the relationship earlier, it's simply a matter of arranging the parts of the relationship from least important to most important. Begin saying good-bye to the part that is least important and move to the most important parts.

I suggest saying good-bye aloud to the person who was lost. Vocalizing the good-bye adds definiteness to what you are doing. Addressing the missing person is very logical. You may intellectually accept the reality of loss, but you don't accept it on other levels. For all practical purposes that missing person still lives with you. Addressing the missing person brings acceptance on all levels.

Some people can review a part of the relationship and say good-bye audibly, others find it easier to write the good-bye first and then read it aloud. Each person must find a way that is best for him or her.

I will share a few cases that illustrate this process.

Barbara lost her husband in a freak accident. Over a year later she was depressed and unable to care for her family.

My sessions with her were so painful that she often left the room and refused to return. Eventually she reviewed and reconstructed her relationship during our sessions.

Day after day she wrote good-bye to parts of the relationship and read them aloud. After covering every part of the relationship she felt it important to say a general good-bye.

Her friend called me to say that Barbara was hysterical, so I went to see her. She was sitting in a chair with a listless expression of her face. She was exhausted. In her hand she held her journal.

"I said my final good-bye," she said quietly.

She looked up at me. A faint smile broke out on her face. "Do you want me to read it to you?"

"Barbara, I'm so happy for your progress. Please read it," I urged.

"Oh, my God, Johnnie...you are dead. You are dead. I will never see you again in this life. Until that day when we meet again, good-bye Johnnie. Good-bye Johnnie. I love you. You know, God, I don't know you very well, but when I get things straightened out I'd like to get to know you better. OK?"

Barbara leaned her head back against the cushion and cried. After the tears stopped, she sighed and quietly said, "I'm glad I'm finally finished."

The next day she went shopping for groceries and cleaned the house thoroughly. She cooked the first good meal in many months. After the meal was over, she gathered her three children close to her. "Children," she lovingly said, "your Momma has spent the last year living for herself. Now I'm going to live for you. Together we're going to be happy again."

A week later Barbara, who had once been very angry with God, asked, "Larry, have you a Bible I can use? Maybe you can tell me where to read to get to know God."

Margie's husband died suddenly during an athletic event. Months later she was harvesting corn in the garden. It suddenly struck her that she and Ed had planted that corn together in the spring.

She reviewed the entire experience in her mind. Going to the store for the seeds and fertilizer, planting the long rows, covering the seeds and finally hoeing the weeds...all of this was reviewed.

Right there in the garden Margie looked up at the blue sky. With hot tears running down her cheeks, she cried, "Ed, Honey? Ed, my dear! You and I planted this corn in the springtime, but we'll never plant corn again in this life. Good-bye to planting corn in the springtime. Good-bye, Ed, to planting corn in the springtime."

Margie told me, "I stood in that corn field and cried for a good half an hour. When I was all through crying, I felt a little space inside of me for something other than constant thoughts of Ed. I had a new freedom that I hadn't felt since before Ed died."

Margie continued saying good-bye until she was ready to move away from her grief entirely. There will be some parts of the relationship that she will need to say good-bye to several times before the pain mellows. This is especially true of the most intimate parts of the relationship.

If peace and healing don't come after a few good-byes to a given part of the relationship, be persistent in saying good-bye until the acute pain eases. It will ease.

Saying good-bye is painful. You will find a hundred reasons not to do it. Do not give in to your reasons. Begin saying goodbye even when you don't want to.

This is the part of grieving that most people resist adamantly. Resistance hinders healing.

Begin saying good-bye. Until you do, you'll be unable to say hello to new relationships with God or people.

Say good-bye. Then say hello to a new chapter of your life. You may not like the chapter you write, but ultimately you'll look back and see some meaning in what your life has written.

Reflection Time

Complete after *Passages...through grief* session

Date: _____

What event or experience had an impact on you at the session tonight?

What feelings, thoughts, or insights did you notice?

What was helpful?

What were your feeling(s) in the closing circle?

Reflection Time

Date: _____

Think about your day today. What is a feeling you have felt (use "Feelings Chart" if help is needed for recognition)?

What event or experience had an impact on you?

What have you done for yourself?

Your thoughts or reactions:

Session Five

Session Five Information for Leaders

Passages Foundations (45 minutes)

Welcome
Moment of silence to recognize their courage
Invite participants to the pot-luck meal next week at _____. (Optional)

- Pass around sign-up sheet for meal contributions

Review **Charting Our Relationship** p. 146 (PM p. 90)

- Ask participants how this exercise was for them

Review and discuss **Forgiveness is...** p. 178

- Clarify understanding
- Refer to **Grieving the Unloved** p. 15
- Refer to **Forgiveness and Healing** p. 173

Review **My Letter of Declaration** instructions p. 181 and format p. 182

- Refer to *Thoughts for My Letter of Declaration* p. 172
- Clarify understanding
- Have participants begin writing their letter in group (5-10 minutes)

Break (5 minutes)

At end of break, each facilitator gathers their sharing group members and move to their meeting space

- Members are to take their mementos
- Facilitators take the **Affirmation** poster

Sharing Group(s) (45 minutes)

Read aloud together the **Affirmation** poster
Invite participants to share their mementos

- For those who have not brought a memento, ask them to share a memory.

If the group needs guidance, offer discussion of:

- Small steps – what steps have they taken?
- What is it like for you at this time?

Reassemble the Whole Group (25 minutes)

- Review "**Letting Go**" article p. 186 (PM p. 125)
- Refer to **Letting Go** p. 174
- Clarify understanding of the article

Complete **Letting Go** ritual p. 175

- Leader gives instructions: "You are invited, in silence, to write to <u>someone</u> any statement or expression you'd like to let go of this evening. When you are ready, place the sheet in the basket. It will be burned with others later—for release."

Leader reads **Guided Visualization** p. 176

In Closing (5 minutes)

Gather Participants in a closing circle
Closing Ritual - invite participants to "Name a feeling you've felt tonight." To create a quiet and accepting atmosphere, join hands and close eyes.

- One leader begins by stating a feeling
- Allow for silence
- Do not expect everyone to participate
- Conclude after appropriate length of silence for sharing by saying, "Go in peace."

Post Session Meeting for Leaders and Facilitators

Letting Go ritual – How was it for them?

What leader(s) would be available to serve as a sounding board to hear the letter of a participant?

Prepare weekly letters for each participant

- Arrange for mailing

Discuss arrangements for the pot-luck meal

Provide support for each other!

Sign-up for the Pot Luck Meal on

_____

Name	Item you will be bringing

Thoughts for "My Letter of Declaration"

The final assignment brings the participant to the place of creating a letter within the form "My Letter of Declaration" (5-6). Writing this letter is the most difficult task of *Passages...through grief.* Participants say it is unforgettable. Hopefully, this is true. By declaring specifically the regrets and difficulties and "wish I'd said" statements, the person is usually making clear, for the first time, what is so vital and unfinished for them. These are the words that need to be said cleanly in order to complete the loss of that particular person or situation. The result for them is immediate. They know they have accomplished something meaningful and really important. They can recognize their courage. It is amazing to observe.

During the Session Six, participants are given the opportunity to read their letters aloud in sharing group. This voicing of their declarations is tremendously reinforcing for their goals of *Passages...through grief.* It also has power for the listening participants. Hopefully, it will be a spur to those who have been reluctant to complete the assignment.

Forgiveness and Healing

Forgiveness is the major focus of Session Five. "Forgiveness is..." replaces the "Grief is..." article. Like the difficult feelings of anger and guilt covered in the previous session, we have found that a struggle to forgive hampers healing. It often marks a compromised quality of life the griever reports.

At the beginning of the presentation, we seek to clarify terms that confound comprehending the process, words like "reconciliation" and "regrets." Next, we use often-misunderstood synonyms which build resentment and can block forgiving. Then we acknowledge how unconstructive attitudes flow from irrational beliefs. Finally, we arrive at the crux of the matte—the willingness to allow forgiveness and healing to take place. Throughout this presentation, participants commonly arrive at an understanding of the material they can latch on to, and frequently verbalize wanting to use the suggestions for themselves. This approach to dealing with forgiveness is novel for most people (i.e., getting away from a religious-toned discussion). It offers them a sense of control in being able to enter into a forgiveness process that can work for them practically and personally.

Letting Go

"Letting go" is a term used for the process of releasing an attitude, a feeling, or a memory that has been painful for us. In the grief process, we frequently get caught up in trying to make sense or justify the loss, so it can be understood. Our thinking goes, "If I figure it out, it won't hurt so much." For it is so difficult to reckon with helplessness. So we chew on it and we chew on it. Letting go occurs, when we finally accept the helplessness and relinquish the power and the situation that has held us in anguish—and held us hostage to the pain. It may be thought of as releasing the attachment to someone else's behavior (like wishing ___ would love me the way I need to be loved). Letting go, I release control. In this relinquishing, letting go parallels the forgiveness process, as we willingly move beyond the stuck place by releasing and facing life from a new direction.

There is a brief article in the participants' manual to support the understanding of "letting go." It seeks to encourage folks to become willing to allow release, which we note is often the only control grievers have. It is suggested that the leader offer a concise description just before the letting go ritual. Then forms are distributed, filled out, folded, and placed in a basket that is returned to the leader. The group is then taken through some moments of deep breathing and a Guided Visualization (LG – 5-5). As members quietly conclude the visualization, the leader proceeds in silence to place the forms in a fire-proof container and allow them to burn to ashes as everyone watches. This enactment is tender and powerful for many, and the silence seems to underscore its value. At the close of this session, participants may well want to have a hug offered.

Participants are reminded that letting go happens in the mind and with intention. They may find this helpful at other times, when they need to let go of something or they want to more completely release what they worked on at this time.

Leaders, as a reminder, practice both the "Letting Go" ritual (burning) and the "Guided Visualization" prior to the session. This practice will provide for a smooth and even voice toned reading and experience.

Letting Go

What I'd like to release now...

_____

_____

_____

Letting Go

What I'd like to release now...

_____

_____

_____

Letting Go

What I'd like to release now...

_____

_____

_____

Guided Visualization

The latter part of Session Five is dedicated to a releasing ceremony. As this experience is meant to be solemn and meaningful, the participants are led through several steps toward release of an important feeling or situation. After a brief discussion of how difficult it is to let go and release, a "Letting Go" sheet (LG -5-6) is handed out for participants to complete. Subsequently, the sheets are collected in a basket and a guided visualization ensues. Once relaxed and breathing quietly, participants are asked to imagine themselves in a quiet and peaceful place in nature. Suggestions are made to gradually notice the sights, sounds and smells of their surroundings.

The text of the guided visualization follows with leader saying:

"Relax, close your eyes, take 3 deep breaths inhaling peace and exhaling stress/strain."

READ VERY SLOWLY:

"Go to a safe place in nature...sit and notice your surroundings...how peaceful this place is. // Gradually, you notice people who have loved you moving into your space...smiling at you. You stand in the center and they surround you. // Their arms are outstretched, offering love to you. Your heart is warmed. You thank them for the love you've been given. From them flow yarn fibers that are knit to create a colorful shawl that surrounds you... encircling you with care and warmth and reassurance. This is a shawl of healing for your spirit. Breath in deeply the calm...the love...the peace...the wholeness meant for you.// You can take this with you...you can take this with you as you quietly come back to this room. Slowly, you will notice the chair beneath you and gradually you will open your eyes...to experience this present moment."

Leader burns "Letting Go" sheets in crockery (lined with heavy foil) in silence.

Take care and offer hugs.

Session Five Guide for Participants

Follow-up for the Week:

Complete *My Letter of Declaration*
Review *Small Steps*
Read Yeagley's article:
    "Walls that Close In"
Use *Reflection Time* notes to support your writing for the week
Our next session will begin at _____ with the Pot-Luck Dinner! (Optional)

Forgiveness is...

When learning about the grief healing process, a connection surfaces that grieving and forgiveness have real overlapping elements. Further readings, personal writing, and memories by grievers can open the way to an understanding of forgiveness that can be <u>useful</u> in an everyday way of living.

First, we need to differentiate some terms we use in order to make forgiveness clearer. Forgiveness is a process we can go through on our own. It is not reconciliation, which involves another person who may or may not be willing to join in the work of forgiveness.

Then, there is forgiveness and there is regret. A couple of specific examples clarify the difference: Forgiveness would be involved if a drunk driver killed someone you loved. In fact, in order to move forward with your life, you would need to release the pain, hate, or resentment toward that alcoholic person. You would need to forgive them, a kind of healing. Whereas, regret would be involved if you realized you had unintentionally chosen career success over family. You would feel regret upon recognizing that the time and energy spent working had robbed you of family experiences and satisfying friendships. Forgiveness and regret. Both powerful, but different.

When asking people what forgiveness means to them, we have heard descriptions that include numerous "shoulds": "If I'm a Christian I should forgive easily" or "I'm OK now...I should be past this!" Actually, the components of forgiveness we most often use include ideas like these, which are quite **<u>unsuitable</u>** for healing a painful hurt. The dictionary's synonyms are words like condone, overlook or excuse... none of which really represent what is meant by forgiveness.

The Process of Forgiveness by William A. Meninger is helpful. In particular, he emphasizes that a big part of coming to forgiveness has to do with understanding what forgiveness is **NOT**. Let us spend some moments considering this list to clarify further.

What Forgiveness is NOT

In the dictionary the word "forgive" is almost adjacent to "forget." In fact, many of us link up forgive and forget, don't we? So,

First, Forgiveness is <u>Not</u>

Forgetting—Actually it's quite the opposite. Forgiveness is a mindfulness of the scar of an emotional wound and its value for our life. When we have learned and grown from the pain's lesson, we can then release the pain. So we do not forgive and forget. We forgive and remember - without the pain.

So, forgiveness is **not a sign of weakness. It is a sign of strength and growth**— where we no longer need anger and resentment to protect us; our memory and love and freedom will equip us for taking care of life.

Second, Forgiveness is Not

Condoning—What happened to us was not okay and it is important not to minimize what happened. A part of healing involves reminding oneself that what happened was wrong, **not okay**. It should not have happened.

In a similar vein, forgiveness is **not absolution**. To absolve can be seen as "letting someone off the hook." It is not our task to answer for someone else. The other person who has done the harm must answer for their own actions. So we do not forgive for their sake, but for our own sake. We forgive so we can get on with life... leaving the baggage behind. We forgive so we can live unencumbered.

Third, Forgiveness is <u>Not</u>

A once-and-for-all decision—Even when forgiveness has taken place freely through healing, hurt can be triggered again by events or memories. At such a time when the painful thought arises, what does this mean? I might say, "Haven't I let go of all that?" However, a re-visitation of pain does not usually last so long or feel so very intense as it once did. That is, *IF* we do not insist on chewing on it.

Finally, pain cannot be willed away. It tends to fade. And forgiveness is not some heroic acceptance...gritting our determined teeth, swallowing hard and saying, "Of course, I forgive her... that's what I have to do." Rather, forgiveness occurs with us as a by-product of healing. And healing is a process that requires time and actions. Healing forgiveness BEGINS with our willingness to let go. Again... healing forgiveness BEGINS with our willingness to let go.

The Starting Point

We come to what is considered step one, **the willingness to forgive**. It sounds simple enough. Stop, recall a time when you had someone to forgive for something very important to you. Remember that pain, that resentment? Remember how you felt justified in being angry? Maybe feeling so-o-o righteous? Now we can recall where we have to start. Step one, the willingness to forgive. Simple? Yes. Difficult? Very.

Step one, when I come to say, "I anguish over this resentment and my self- righteous glee at how awful that other person is who hurt me. I do long to be released from this nagging obsession. My longing is for a clean heart and a peaceful spirit."

179

Forgiveness of others, as well as ourselves, can be problematic. For example, there was a teenage girl who ran away from home for several months. During her absence, her parents worked hard to understand their daughter's perspective and hear her needs. By the time she returned home, they had reached a place of forgiveness, acceptance, and loving welcome for her. However, it took the young woman years to receive their gift and forgive herself. So it often is for us; we might be able to forgive someone else, but have difficulty forgiving ourselves.

There are different kinds of situations that call for forgiveness. Some are small or every day, like feeling left out of a group you long to be a part of. This calls for forgiving other's oversight and thoughtlessness. Or, there is the forgiveness of life for its disillusionments, such as forgiving oneself at 45 for not being the big success you expected to be in your 20s. A number of forgiveness needs arise out of our own expectations of the way things are supposed to be, or the way people should treat us. These are called irrational beliefs, ideas we have decided on in our own heads. We need to recognize these viewpoints, look at the actual situation, and decide whether they are useful or need to be released.

When one family traveled to Italy, they visited the Accademia Galleria in Florence where Michelangelo's sculpture of the David is housed. Before reaching the super-sized statue, they passed through an anteroom that housed large chunks of stone, most with partially sculpted figures emerging from them. Describing the artistic process, Michelangelo stated that when he searched for marble to use, he found himself hunting for the image that wanted to be released from it. The stone material seemed to know what it wanted to be. In other words, he saw sculpting as an excavation project, bringing forth that hidden figure. Michelangelo's artistic process seems applicable to much of spiritual and emotional life. By chipping away at the thoughts and habits, and yes, places of non-forgiveness that interfere with our wholeness, we are released to become who we are meant to be.

What we want you to know is that on the other side of forgiveness there is a powerful sense of release. It sets you free, really free!

"My Letter of Declaration" Instructions

Writing "My Letter of Declaration" is a **very** valuable tool to help you say words or declare feelings that you have not been able to do in person. The words you write are for **your use**—be honest. Do not mail the letter. Rather, save it to remind you of your ability to make a difference for yourself in an incomplete relationship.

Where you find the blank line, write in the name you used for the person.

_____, *I regret:* these statements are to acknowledge situations you wish you could have handled differently.

_____, *I recognize that you:* these statements are to declare the difficulty you have had with that person.

_____, *it is important to me that you know*: these statements declare thoughts that you long to have the person hear.

_____, *in order to take care of myself, I strive to:* these statements of self-care or letting go provide you with the opportunity to reclaim your personal power.

Use a closing statement that fits you and your relationship. Some examples could be:

- I Love You,
- I Miss You,
- I need to say goodbye for my own sake,
- It is time for me to move on,
- Finally,

Sign your name after your closing statement.

Complete your letter and bring it with you to the final session of *Passages...through grief*. You will be given an opportunity to share the letter with those in your sharing group. Reading the letter aloud gives the words power and release for you. If you choose not to share your letter during *Passages...through grief*, do share it with someone. Choose a person who will just listen with acceptance and recognize your courage. When you complete the reading, celebrate (hugs allowed)! If you do not have a trusted someone for sharing your declarations, ask a leader of *Passages...through grief*, a chaplain, or a professional to listen.

Feel free to use this format to approach another incomplete relationship you identified on "Charting the Relationship."

My Letter of Declaration

Dear _____ (name you called the person),

    I have spent valuable time and effort thinking about our relationship, and there are some things I need to declare to you.

_____, I regret ...

_____, I regret ...

_____, I regret ...

_____, I recognize that you...

_____, I recognize that you...

_____, I recognize that you ...

_____, it is important to me that you know ...

_____, it is important to me that you know ...

_____, it is important to me that you know...

_____, in order to take care of myself, I strive to ...

_____, in order to take care of myself, I strive to ...

_____, in order to take care of myself, I strive to ...

Letting Go

"Letting go" is a term used for the process of releasing an attitude, a feeling or a memory that has been painful for us. In the grief process we frequently get caught up in trying to make sense of the loss or justify it, so it can be understood. Our thinking goes, "If I figure it out, it won't hurt so much." For it is so difficult to reckon with helplessness. So we chew on it and we chew on it. Letting go occurs when we finally accept the helplessness and relinquish the power and the situation that has held us in anguish...and held us "hostage" to the pain. It is frequently associated with releasing the attachment to someone else's behavior (like wishing _____ would love me the way I need to be loved). Letting go, I release control. In this relinquishing, letting go parallels the forgiveness process as we willingly move beyond the stuck place. We release, turn, and face life from a new direction.

Letting go happens in the mind and with our intention. During this session we are setting aside a time to focus on something important to us that needs to be released. We name it and write it down. We remind ourselves that we long to be released from this burden emotionally and spiritually. By this acknowledgement, we are preparing ourselves for release. Pay attention to the steps taken in the ritual we do together. It may be helpful later when you know that you need to let go of something, or you want to more completely release what you worked on this time. Feel free to use the space below to note what steps were taken and how this experience was for you...so you can repeat it.

_____

_____

_____

_____

_____

Yeagley's

"Walls That Close In"

A 30-year-old woman struggled to get the words out. Slowly she said, "You'll never know how I long for someone to touch me. Someone to hold me. Just anyone. I thought we had a good marriage. It seemed like it to me. Little did I know that just weeks after the honeymoon he was seeing another woman. We stayed together for six months – long enough for me to get pregnant. Now my daughter is five. Just the two of us. She is a doll, but when it is all said and done, I am alone. I can't cling to her for my emotional support. It isn't fair. Every night I long to be in someone's arms. The desire for someone to touch me and say 'I love you' overpowers me. I feel the four walls of that house closing in on me. In desperation, I bury my face in a pillow and cry until I fall asleep. Somehow, somewhere, there must be an answer for me."

Several people in the group were moved to tears and to action when they heard her cry for help. They went over to her and embraced her and spoke quiet words of comfort.

These were words of loneliness – symbols of painful loss. Every person in the group felt an aching of heart cried out, "Something must be done."

A distraught mother fumbled with the doily on the arm of the couch in an effort to tell me her story without weeping. "He was so young and full of life. His great love was riding his bicycle. His bicycle took him to his death. You see, he rode it out onto the ice. We don't know if he fell and the weight of the fall broke the ice or whether he just hit a weak place in the ice. He didn't have a chance."

"Now I go into his bedroom and sit for a long time. I try to remember his voice and see his face when he was excited about something. I wait, thinking that maybe he'll just walk into the room and say, 'Hi Mom,' but he never does. I know I have the other children, and my husband has been real good, but this house is so empty. I feel so alone."

The loneliness of this mother still tugs at my heart.

Loneliness seems to be a pre-packaged ingredient of grief. I have yet to meet a person who hasn't experienced it. There are some who go so far as to say that loneliness is a part of being human apart from grief. Others feel that there are chapters of loneliness that fit into every maturational stage of life ranging from loneliness due to birth to loneliness due to the abandonment of the aged.

I have learned from grieving people that loneliness hits you the hardest months after the funeral or divorce. They taught me that during the first few months of grief people are too busy being angry, guilty or numb with shock and denial to be lonely. When they care for all the business related to the separation and express the hostility against the doctors or family – then comes the incomparable loneliness of grief.

It has become obvious to me that when people do not fight grief, but let it happen as a normal human reaction to a great loss, they have sufficient coping power to manage their loneliness. The sooner and more intensely grieving is done in the early months after the loss, the easier it becomes to handle the situation of being alone.

If grieving people have adequate support systems during early grief, they very likely will have developed new and renewed relationships that will soften the blow of being alone.

Loneliness results from the sudden removal of a person's source of satisfaction of human hungers. That satisfaction can only take place via intimate personal relationships.

Over and over the participants of grief recovery programs insist that you have to make up your mind that loneliness will not rule your life. That may be "easier said than done," but a lot of people have done it. Let me share some of the secrets they have shared with me.

Do your grieving early and intensely.

You don't have to be strong for others. You are not obligated to get back to normal so that others are comfortable around you. Grief is a sign that you are healing and growing as a person. Let it happen.

After a reasonable length of intense grief, say good-bye to the relationship that was lost.

It is a psychological amputation that is vital to your overall health. Some people keep a journal and say good-bye in the journal. Others say good-bye to things they did with the person while holding his or her picture in front of them. Saying good-bye is a healthy closure to the period of intense grief.

Some of the comments I hear reveal the value of this closure.

"Once I said good-bye to doing everything with Ned, I had the best day since he died. It was like a heavy responsibility had been lifted off my shoulders."

"After I wrote my farewell to Jim, I told my kids that we had been living in the past. Now we were going to live for each other and do things to make our lives count. I cleaned the house that day and we all ate a good supper."

"I said good-bye. Along with the good-bye came a release from the anger I had toward God and I wanted to get to know Him."

Begin to concentrate on your own life.

Set short-term goals for using your talents and for developing new ones. Gradually, break habit patterns based upon "the two of us" and move from the world of "we" into the world of "I." Build your self-identity and do things that you like to do. If you and your children are survivors from the death of a spouse, plan some things for the new-sized family. Make a calendar of events.

Look at solitude as a friend.

This is time for self-confrontation. Who am I? What can I become? How do I view life – as a drudge, a right or a gift? What are my values? Do I like myself? What areas of my life can I improve? Am I a giver or a taker? These are a few of the self-confrontational questions that can turn your solitude into growth adventures.

Become knowledgeable about the world around you.

Broaden your interests and be well-read. This expands the inner person. A variety of challenging activities will make you an interesting person and put you in touch with interesting people. This is a good way to combat loneliness that leads to despair.

Volunteer your time.

Some people may find volunteering an effective preventive measure against loneliness. It depends on the person and on the type of service for which you are volunteering.

Grief produces fatigue.

For this reason a person should get adequate rest, plan a balanced diet and do plenty of big muscle exercise. Instead of wearing old sweats all the time, wear something that uplifts your spirits. You'll feel good about yourself. A person who feels good about his or her appearance will find it easier to reach out to others.

Loneliness often becomes a way of life for those who live in the past. Reliving the experiences of yesteryear robs the energy that could be used to make each day a new chapter. Take from the past the lessons of value and then go beyond the achievements of days gone by.

The regrets of the past cannot be changed. Nobody has a chance for a rerun. All we can do is learn from our mistakes and try to make the present count.

I received a card from an Oscar Smith. He checked the box marked, "I desire to know more about the Scriptures." Thinking I was about to meet a young man with very little knowledge of the Bible, I rang the doorbell and waited eagerly.

I suddenly heard a voice behind me. "Yes, what can I do for you?"

I turned and saw an old man with a cane in his hand. I told him I was responding to his card. His eyes twinkled as he invited me to his upstairs apartment.

"I have a great deal to learn and such a short time to learn it in. I know of the work of your church only slightly, but I must know more. Teach me all you can. I am open for more understanding," he pleaded.

Who was Oscar? A 99-year-old retired minister who had been preaching since he was 17. His wife had died five years earlier. Loneliness came to be his guest, but Oscar couldn't take time to entertain it. It soon left.

His dining room table was covered with correspondence and research papers in the process of being written. Several times a week he was taken to dinners for senior citizens where he served as the chaplain. His one goal was to bring Christians of <u>all</u> faiths into unity.

I attended Oscar's 100th birthday celebration at a senior citizen center. With interest I listened to the 10-minute sermon he had been preparing for some time. It was a masterpiece – the reading of the text, statement of purpose, three points, summary and application. His timing was exactly 10 minutes. He didn't have a single note from which to speak.

A middle-aged minister sitting next to me leaned over and whispered, "That old man makes my preaching sound sick."

My response was, "The reason he can preach so well at 100 is because he never stopped living."

Oscar was hospitalized just before he had his 100th birthday. This was a great concern to him because he was scheduled to make a presentation of books to the library of his alma mater. Catheterization was no obstacle to Oscar. On the morning of the presentation he talked the physician into giving him a 10-hour pass. The proper attachments were supplied and off he went to his seminary. By supper he was back in his hospital bed.

Oscar and I were like brothers. He shared with me the secret of creatively living alone. First of all he suffered from the death of his wife, but he concluded that life is a gift from God. In his grief he thanked God for sharing the life of a woman with him.

While Oscar didn't invite his great loss, he looked at grief as an experience of growth. He sought ways of adjusting that would dynamically change him from within.

He decided very early that once he worked his way through his grief, he would not be captive to the feelings of grief the rest of his life. He believed that we feel the way we choose to feel.

Within months of his wife's death, Oscar began to reach out to others. His willingness to learn and lift others up drew me to the old man. He soothed my troubled heart. His ministry to my soul cemented our relationship, guaranteeing Oscar that he would never be hopelessly lonely.

Oscar taught me that grief is like a picture projected out of focus on a screen. The larger objects can be made out with much effort, but the tiny details are completely lost in the blur. Recovery is the turning of the lens that brings the picture into focus. As the focus sharpens, all the little details stand out in a way that complements the larger objects. In the end we can look at the whole with new appreciation.

Walls close in on those who refuse to reach out and dialogue with others.

Reflection Time

Complete after *Passages...through grief* session

Date: _____

What event or experience had an impact on you at the session tonight?

What feelings, thoughts, or insights did you notice?

What was helpful?

What were your feeling(s) in the closing circle?

Reflection Time

Date: _____

Think about your day today. What is a feeling you have felt (use "Feelings Chart" if help is needed for recognition)?

What event or experience had an impact on you?

What have you done for yourself?

Your thoughts or reactions:

Session Six

Session Six Information for Leaders

Dinner (45 minutes)

Enjoy the companionship of this social time!

Passages Foundations (45 minutes)

Complete *Passages...through grief* Program Evaluation pp. 197, 199 (PM p. 139)

- Refer to **Evaluation Form** p. 196
- Reinforce the need for honesty in responses
- Collect for leader's review after session

Complete **Depression Symptoms Scale** p. 202 (PM p. 142)

- Ask, "What changes have you noticed in your scale results?"
- Refer to **Red Flags** p. 7

Extend an open invitation to:

- Repeat *Passages...through grief* should they find it useful for their journey
- Use forms to explore other unresolved relationships (additional forms provided at the end of the participant's manual)

Participants move to their sharing groups (5 minutes)

- Facilitators take the **Affirmation** poster

Sharing Group(s) (45 minutes)

Read aloud together the **Affirmation** poster
Discuss **My Letter of Declaration** p. 182 (PM p. 121)

- Ask, "What was this experience like for you?"
- Invite participants to share their letters

- Offer encouragement to share, not pressure. Note how valuable it is to have witnesses.

Optional Activity: invite members to offer positive feedback to each other. Examples:

- Something a person has taken to task
- Something a person has done well
- Courage another has exhibited

In Closing (15 minutes)

Introduce **A Gift to Myself** p. 203 (PM p. 143)

- Invite participants to begin completing **A Gift** (5 minutes)
- Encourage them to complete it following the Session

Read aloud **Grief is...** p. 205 (PM p. 145)
Leader reads "**Imperfections**" p. 206 (PM p. 146)
Gather participants in a closing circle
Closing ritual – invite participants to "Name a **strength** you have gained through our time together."

- Allow for silence
- Do not expect everyone to participate
- Conclude with "Go in peace."

Offer hugs of congratulations!

Post Session Meeting for Leaders and Facilitators

Review and discuss **Program Evaluations**

- Note suggested changes
- Celebrate what has worked well!

Conclude business/loose ends—examples:

- Scheduling the next *"Passages...through grief"* program

Appreciate yourself for having accepted the challenge of accompanying these persons on their journey!

Evaluation Form

During the final session, following the shared meal, the participants are asked to complete a "Program Evaluation" p. 199. They are told that their input has helped in the evolution of **Passages...through grief,** and continues to benefit those who will participate in the future. After the form is filled out, the remainder of the session is begun. As leaders, we have found that the input of participants is both supportive for us and quite valuable for modifying our presentations. Examples of comments from the past are offered for use in promoting the series (p. 46).

Session Six Guide for Participants

Additional Forms for Your Use:

Passages...through grief
Program Evaluation

In order to meet the needs of those we serve through *Passages...through grief,* your honest evaluation of the program is needed. We welcome both constructive criticism and positive comments. You do not need to sign your name if you would rather keep your evaluation confidential. **Thank you for your help!**

Date: _____

Please comment on the following (feel free to continue on the back of the page):

	What was helpful?	What was not helpful?
Educational information presented at the beginning of each session		
Open discussion times		
Weekly printed notes and readings		

"Sharing Group" experience		
Meditations and guided visualization		
Information and use of *"Forgiveness Is..."*		
Using "Reflection Time"		
Weekly "Follow-up" assignments		

Suggestions of what you would like to add to the program:

When I think of *Passages...through grief* I will remember:

What would you share with others about this experience?

Other comments.....

Depression Symptoms Scale

Date: _____

Place a check under the number that indicates where you think you fit at this time.

0 = no problem   **10 = big problem**

Symptom	0	1	2	3	4	5	6	7	8	9	10
Tired most of the time											
General feeling of weakness											
Worried about the next thing you must do.											
Crying/tearfulness											
Poor memory											
Loss of self-esteem											
Changes in sleep pattern											
Agitated, restless, tense											
Overwhelming sadness											
Feeling unworthy or guilty											
Unable to concentrate											
Feelings of abandonment											
Changes in eating pattern											
Lost interest in former pleasant activities											

A Gift to Myself

This program has been focused on recognizing the pain and anguish of loss, gaining skills to meet and deal with feelings, and recognizing what is important to keep or release.

A "new normal" emerges from this process through the gifts you give yourself. Recognize these gifts by answering the following questions.

What "small steps" have I taken?

What strengths have I developed?

What weaknesses have I overcome?

What ways of caring for myself am I now using?

How am I now using my voice to ask for what I need?

What have I let go of or relinquished

What have I discovered about my "new normal?"

Grief is...

As you complete this workshop, you have taken the opportunity to look at your grief and learn tools to make a difference in your recovery. Your future is hopeful, knowing what you now know! A final piece to consider are the terms "strength" and "courage", and how they will lead you in your "new normal".

Let's look at the definitions of these two terms. *The Merriam-Webster Dictionary* (2015 online edition) defines:

- Strength as "the capacity for exertion, endurance, toughness".
- Courage as "mental or moral strength to venture, persevere, and withstand danger, fear, or difficulty".

These terms are NOT interchangeable, as they are sometimes used, but some of both will make your "new normal" more workable. Some thoughts on how they are beneficial...

- ❖ Witnessing the pain of others requires *strength*. Allowing your own pain requires *courage*.
- ❖ Holding in feelings requires *strength*. Being forthcoming with your feelings requires *courage*.
- ❖ Dealing with your needs **alone** requires *strength*. Asking for help requires *courage*.
- ❖ Being inflexible with what you know requires *strength*. Opening your mind and heart to new ideas requires *courage*.
- ❖ Loving others requires *strength*. Opening yourself to accepting love requires *courage*.

May you use the courage within you to make your "new normal" free to love and live fully.

Imperfections

by Lindsey Coombs

Getting glued together
after being broken
does not leave me
whole again. I am
put back with cracks,

like the plate on the mantel,
the sugar bowl in the kitchen,
the rabbit still missing
part of an ear, I've been
chipped and broken

and learned to love more
for all the carelessness,
for seeing creation
with all its imperfections,
for forgiving myself
and this crazy broken world
over and over again.

In Closing

As you come to the conclusion of this manual, we hope you recognize the hard work you have done. Your grief process continues. You have been offered understandings and skills that will be useful in continuing to do good things for yourself toward healing. We once wrote a compassion card that said, "Time does not heal all wounds. It takes time to do healing things." In that light, we encourage you to congratulate yourself on your journey and support yourself in doing healing things.

Reflection Time

Date: _____

Think about your day today. What is a feeling you have felt (use "Feelings Chart" if help is needed for recognition)?

What event or experience had an impact on you?

What have you done for yourself?

Your thoughts or reactions:

Charting Our Relationship Graph

My relationship with ———————

Beginning ——————————————————————————— Today

My Letter of Declaration

Dear _____ (name you called the person),

    I have spent valuable time and effort thinking about our relationship, and there are some things that I need to declare to you.

_____, I regret ...

_____, I regret ...

_____, I regret ...

_____, I recognize that you...

_____, I recognize that you...

_____, I recognize that you ...

_____, it is important to me that you know ...

_____, it is important to me that you know ...

_____, it is important to me that you know...

_____, in order to take care of myself, I strive to ...

_____, in order to take care of myself, I strive to ...

_____, in order to take care of myself, I strive to ...

Letting Go

What I'd like to release now...

_____

_____

_____

Letting Go

What I'd like to release now...

_____

_____

_____

Letting Go

What I'd like to release now...

_____

_____

_____

Printed in the USA
CPSIA information can be obtained
at www.ICGtesting.com
LVHW070023280124
770147LV00013B/1334